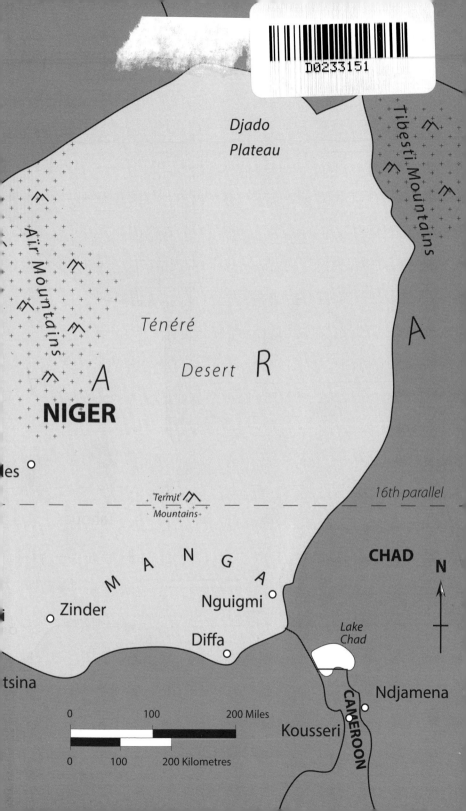

D0233151

Alistair Carr is a Fellow of the Royal Geographical Society, and is author of *The Singing Bowl – Journeys through Inner Asia*. He lives in Suffolk with his wife.

Essex County Council

3013020791129 7

'A brave, unusual and ambitious journey, in the old style of travel that I (of course) welcome. I've never been to any part of the Sahel. But this made me want to go.' **Colin Thubron**

'A remarkable and tenacious adventure in the finest tradition of British travel writing. Alistair Carr sheds light on a troubled and long-neglected part of the world that will occupy policymakers for years to come.' **Justin Marozzi**

'Carr's prose can be wonderfully evocative'. *TLS*

THE NOMAD'S PATH

TRAVELS IN THE SAHEL

ALISTAIR CARR

I.B. TAURIS

LONDON · NEW YORK

Published in 2014 by I.B.Tauris & Co Ltd
6 Salem Road, London W2 4BU
175 Fifth Avenue, New York NY 10010
www.ibtauris.com

Distributed in the United States and Canada Exclusively by Palgrave Macmillan
175 Fifth Avenue, New York NY 10010

Copyright © 2014 Alistair Carr

The right of Alistair Carr to be identified as the author of this work has been
asserted by him in accordance with the Copyright, Designs and Patents Act
1988.

All rights reserved. Except for brief quotations in a review, this book, or any
part thereof, may not be reproduced, stored in or introduced into a retrieval
system, or transmitted, in any form or by any means, electronic, mechanical,
photocopying, recording or otherwise, without the prior written permission
of the publisher.

ISBN: 978 1 78076 689 8

A full CIP record for this book is available from the British Library
A full CIP record is available from the Library of Congress

Library of Congress Catalog Card Number: available

Typeset by 4word Ltd, Bristol
Printed and bound in Sweden by ScandBook AB

CONTENTS

ILLUSTRATIONS

Maps

ACKNOWLEDGEMENTS

F irst and foremost, I would like to thank my guides: Omar and Ahmet. My life was in their hands for the duration of our journey across the Manga. I am also immensely grateful for the hospitality given to us by all the Tubu we stayed with along the way. Thank you to Leslie Clark, Charlene Pidgeon and Peroji for the travels with the Wodaaabe, and to Richard Grail for letting me stay in his Agades home. Thanks also to Carol Beckwith, Professor Jeremy Keenan, Professor Harry Norris and Dr Amira Bennison; to the late Paul Marsh, my agent, for being so supportive of this project and to Geraldine Cooke, Stephen Davies and Janice Brent. Thank you, also, to Colin Thubron for helpful manuscript observations.

And, of course, thanks to Sarah for being so wonderfully loving, patient and understanding.

For Sarah

In memory of Ray, Mark and Ross Hanna

INTRODUCTION

A lmost three years had passed since I last heard the tones of a camel growl, when I sat under a leafy trellis in Agades sipping a refrigerated drink of ginger, spices and lemon juice. The muezzin's chant glided across the Saharan town and I listened with contained excitement as Eva Macher, an Austrian in her early fifties, described how there was a vast region to the north-east of Zinder that was untouched by the modern world: few, if any Caucasians, had ever penetrated the place.

'Where you'll be going, and living with the nomads who are there – they're true nomads,' Eva ruminated, as a breeze ruffled the overhead canopy. 'No outside contact at all – you'll never get ill with them.'

'Like the Aborigines,' I replied.

'Exactly,' she remarked, as sunlight splintered into a fistful of diamonds around us. 'But,' she continued, 'I think in three years, even there, that way of life would have disappeared.'

I had not forgotten Niger or its nomads, but this conversation, recorded in my journal during the trip's closing week, had been mislaid among the pages of life's intervening chapters. I had travelled there for the Aïr's rock art. Scientists make copies of petroglyphs in the manner of a brass rubbing, but they mostly use charcoal; I planned to work with colour – oil and soft pastels – with a view to then selling the prehistoric images at a London gallery. The two months I spent in Agades, the Ténéré desert and the Aïr Mountains, with its memories of half-mile-high dust devils, xanthic shades, robed Tuaregs and prickling heat, all seemed a long time ago – but I sensed that I would have to return, because there was a feeling of an incomplete journey.

In my subsequent enquiries into the history of Agades and the role it played in the Old Salt Road, I forgot my own journey and became more interested in those that others had undertaken over the centuries either by choice or unhappy fate. By the time I decided to return to Niger, I had lost sight of north-east Zinder entirely and, instead, hoped to accompany one of the Tuareg salt caravans on the final annual leg of their return journey south from Agades to Katsina – an ancient salt road entrepot in northern Nigeria.

Then I read, with mounting frustration, of the burgeoning Tuareg rebellion that flared up in the Aïr Mountains during February 2007 and, over the next few months, from the safe confines of my Suffolk home, I followed the rebels' progress with a muted sense of dismay. With each new attack – as in June, when the Tuaregs shot up Agades airport, then defeated two columns of government troops in the desert – the likelihood of my return to Niger diminished. Aghaly ag Alambo led the rebels, who called themselves the *Mouvement des Nigériens pour la Justice* (Niger Movement for Justice), or MNJ, and they claimed the government had failed to honour the 1995 peace agreement that ended the first Tuareg rebellion (1990–5). The new rebellion had started, as one source put it, because of 'the culmination of widespread disaffection amongst Tuareg ex-combatants with the slow progress of promised benefits, lack of functioning democratic institutions, and a perceived special status given to foreign mining interests and political leaders.'

The MNJ attacks were making an impact but, for Agades, it was bad news, as the already fickle tourist trade would disappear entirely until the conflict was resolved. Agades, as I remembered – with its lively collage of desert peoples attired in robes, turbans and swords – smelt of baked dust and its back streets had all the disorientating traits of the desert; the narrow alleys, medieval in character, twisted and meandered like a trickle of water pushing its way through a carpet of dust: one alley filtered into another, a left turn, then a right and it all looked the same. There were few trees and little shade in the town, and the September heat sucked the moisture from both the animate and the inanimate; baguettes baked at 6 o'clock in the morning became crusty and brittle by midday and, if squeezed in the hand, would disintegrate into crumbs as temperatures rose to over 100°F in the shade.

By the middle of December, there were ugly stories of summary executions and roadside land mine explosions around Agades. The small Aïr towns of Iferouane and Ingal had been deserted, an embargo had been imposed on the Aïr Mountains and the Ténéré desert, and there was a rumour that the rebels were digging in for a long war and even threatening to cut off Agades. In addition, two French journalists had been arrested in the surrounding desert for trying to make contact with the rebels; they had been given permission by the authorities to be in the south of the country on a bird flu related project, but were discovered in a jeep in the north. Both they and their two guides were subsequently incarcerated in a notorious prison outside Niamey and were being held as a warning to the West and its journalists not to interfere. Yet, despite all this (and my muffled anxieties), I felt it was a case of either going then or never at all; the urge to return was powerful. Somehow, not to do so would have been a failing on my part.

The night before I was due to fly to Niamey, on 9 January 2008, I received a phone call from someone I had met by chance the previous day. He had visited Agades on a few occasions: 'Are you all packed?' he asked.

'Yes,' I replied. 'I'm leaving tomorrow.'

'I've got Céline staying here,' he said. 'She has some views on Niger at this time. I'll pass you over to her.'

Céline and her husband Akly owned the *Auberge d'Azel*, where they spent half the year with their two children and, when I lived in Agades, I often dined in their elegant bougain-villea- and vine-trellised courtyard. '*Salut*, Alistair,' she exclaimed, barely able to disguise her anxiety. '*Ça va?*'

'*Ça va bien. Merci*,' I answered.

'Look,' she said, continuing in French. 'A mine exploded in Niamey last night.'

I paused briefly, absorbing her sentence. '*Les Touareg?*'

'No one knows,' Céline responded. 'The situation is very unstable. The country is basically at war.'

'Can you still get to Agades?'

'Only by military escort, but there are no tourists there... Akly has been based in Niamey since June.'

I told her about my plans to join a Tuareg caravan heading south. 'You should be all right as long as you don't have any hidden agendas,' she warned, in implied reference to the imprisonment of the French journalists.

'I don't.'

'*Alors... Bonne chance.*'

1

The swollen Niger seemed to throb as an amber sun disappeared behind a distant ridge of silhouetted undulations. The bridge across the river was dotted with pedestrians and fleeting traffic and, on the bank's lip at the far side, the shadow of a man stood beside two camels that craned their necks towards the sturdy current.

I sat on *Le Grand Hotel*'s expansive terrace, stirring an ice-filled glass of Coca-Cola with a yellow straw, while listening to Akly talk about the rebellion. Between his animated sentences, I became aware that the white plastic tables around us were slowly being occupied by French expats, mostly men in jackets, as local waiters threaded silently amongst their former colonial masters. There was an agitated sizzling from somewhere behind us, and the air was fragranced with spicy kebabs as dusky shades settled over Niamey and beyond.

The *Institut Géographique National* map of Niger I had bought in London was spread out in front of us, like an unfolded, starched tablecloth, and I watched Akly's index finger skirt along the fringes of the Aïr before circling specific mountainous areas that, from the topography, appeared to resemble vast fortresses.

'There may be,' he observed, 'as many as a thousand rebels equipped with up to forty 4×4s. Most expats with commercial interests in Agades have moved to Niamey,' he continued. '*L'Auberge d'Azel* is open, but I am advising clients not to go. The only customers we've had in the last few months are from either the Red Cross or *Médecins Sans Frontières*.'

'What do you think about travelling south from Agades to Katsina with a Tuareg caravan?' I asked.

'I don't think you should go to Agades,' he advised in rapid French. 'Even if you do get permission you will only arouse suspicion and, if you travel with Tuaregs, you'll be endangering not only your own life but, because you are a white man, theirs too.'

I could not think of an appropriate response, but my glum expression did not require translation. As my eyes roamed over the map, and the areas free of rebel activity beneath Agades, I saw Zinder and, from there, glanced east to a town called Nguigmi on the border with Chad.

'What about here?' I tendered, pointing to the geography north-east of Zinder.

'There has been no reported trouble there, so you should be all right,' Akly replied, peering into the region I had outlined.

'Good,' I murmured. And I remembered a conversation about a forgotten nomadic land that had no contact with the modern world.

Akly, in his early fifties, explained that, as a boy, he spent two years in Nguigmi when the shores of Lake Chad lapped up to the small conurbation at the foot of the Old Salt Road. He remembered fishing its waters, and hunting duck and other game along its lush green banks; today, in one of nature's more recent statements, Lake Chad has receded to such an extent it is now one hundred and fifty kilometres from the town. Akly's French father was a cartographer, who mapped the region to the east of the Aïr Mountains, and his mother was a Tuareg. This genealogical composition was elegantly blended in him: mahogany-coloured eyes and subtly hawkish contours complemented a golden complexion.

We discussed the mine that had exploded two days earlier, the first in the city's history, and I learnt that one person, a journalist, had been killed. Nobody had claimed responsibility, and the Tuareg rebels had sent a missive to the authorities disclaiming any part in it.

'There is such an atmosphere of suspicion with the rebellion and the arrest of the French journalists', Akly observed, 'that mobile phone calls, particularly international ones, are being tapped.'

'I noticed an odd distortion when I rang home earlier – I wondered if that was the reason. Someone must have been listening in.'

I had been aware, before I arrived, that Niamey would probably be smouldering with mistrust and fear, and that was why I had decided to visit the Ministry of Tourism to obtain permission for my travel plans. It seemed the most logical path to make myself transparent with the authorities. In this way, I hoped to defuse any suspicion that might surround a white man travelling in Niger during troubled times. I explained this concept to Akly, as the darkening light conjured its deceptions on the surroundings beyond the illuminated terrace.

'It's a good idea,' he said. 'I know the Director there – Ibrahim. He's a friend of mine. When you go, just tell him that I suggested you speak to him.'

I studied the map and noticed the region to the west of Nguigmi was marked: M A N G A. 'If you do get permission to travel through there,' Akly said following my gaze, 'I think you will discover things.'

2

The television screen, mounted in the corner of *Les Roniers'* small hotel bar, transmitted a French news channel that was dominated by the imprisonment of the two journalists outside Niamey. It seemed that ambassadorial intervention, however graceful, pressured or vociferous, was achieving very little, for the broadcaster announced there was no immediate prospect of their release. I walked through to the restaurant, where tables were set up as if in a Provençal café, and out onto the gravel veranda. A hoopoe was perched on the apex of a wrought iron chair, its head feathers unfurling like a fan in a lady's nimble hand. As I sat down at a garden table in the mottled shade, a couple of native pigeons, invisible in the wandering branches, murmured uninterrupted solos, as if each was deciphering the other's purring notes for the possibility of a hidden invitation.

The grounds surrounding the hotel were testament that the property had once been a private home: the bright lime plumage of long-tailed parakeets could be glimpsed amongst the leaves of the many gnarled acacias, like clownfish hiding in the tentacles of sea anemones, and two white egrets stood motionless beside the swimming pool, their snowy reflections reduced to ghostly forms by a cluster of rogue ripples. Bougainvillea tumbled over a rusting pergola beneath a leafless baobab and the spiky, verdant foliage of palm trees.

The house itself was quite small, and the owners, Annie and Pierre Colas, lived in the rooms above the restaurant, bar and kitchen, while guests were lodged in one of the dozen round huts named after African wildlife. A once-cherished tennis court had been warped by the sun's relentless attention, its surface buckled and cracked. Behind the disintegrating netting, a Wahlberg eagle lifted clumsily into the sky from the tangled canopy of an ageing acacia, and a boy hung a sheet on a taut clothes line outside a sepia-coloured hut.

Apart from the tiny manicured patch of lawn between the restaurant and the swimming pool, there was very little grass and the ground was a carpet of chalky, brown dust inhabited in places by theatres of insect activity. Ants marched in line or scrambled amongst the parched detritus in search of bounty, while olive-green lizards scurried past. A dung beetle pushed a small ball of dirt, its hind legs moving robot-like, while its front tibias worked skilfully to maintain the ball's momentum; and a long-tailed glossy starling settled on an overhanging eucalyptus sprig, as if surveying the scene. A scrawny hedge ran around the perimeter of the grounds and, beneath it, a kindling fence had been erected to separate *Les Roniers*, oasis-like, from its bedraggled surroundings. And you could spot the Niger, glistening like mercury, as it snaked its way through the shimmering landscape.

*   *   *

I wanted to get a second opinion on the rebellion and called Liman, a Tuareg who lived in Agades, but, I knew, was temporarily in Niamey. A few hours later, he arrived at *Les Roniers* and climbed out of a Subaru jeep dressed in a bright green robe and a bulbous white turban. I recognised him from when he had collected me from the bus terminal in Agades. As we sat at a table on the dappled gravel terrace and I listened to him chatter about the rebellion, I became aware of the suspicious glances being cast in our direction by some of the hotel staff. '*C'est pas bon*,' Liman exclaimed, as if on cue, 'for a Tuareg and a European to be seen travelling together at this time.' His eyes seemed to well up with increasing anxiety as he talked about the current troubles in Agades and of the mines that had recently exploded in the region. 'I counsel you,' he advised, 'not to go to Agades.'

From the contorted position in which he was seated, it was obvious Liman was in significant physical discomfort and, in a pause during his assessment of Agades, he described how he had a weak disc and was hoping to have an operation in Mali when he could afford it. Because of problems with my own back, I kept a chiropractic chart, indicating the effects of spinal misalignments, in the pouch of my notebook and, remembering it was there, I removed the sheet and unfolded it.

'Dinosaur!' he exclaimed, as he gazed over the column of vertebrae, in reference to the Cretaceous skeletons and bones he would have seen in the Ténéré desert.

I explained that it was not a dinosaur, but a chart showing how the body's controlling nerves can be disturbed by vertebral misalignments, and that if 6C (the sixth cervical vertebra), for example, was out – which affects neck muscles, shoulders and tonsils – a person might have a stiff neck, pains in the upper arm or tonsillitis. Or if it was the atlas – which affects blood supply to the head – headaches, high blood pressure or chronic tiredness might be experienced. After we tried to correlate some of his pain with our map of the spine, the conversation returned to Agades, and I learned how, even today, salt caravans band together in the Aïr Mountains before crossing the Ténéré as a precaution against bandits.

I told him my thoughts on travelling between Zinder and the Chad border and, like Akly, he observed that there had been no trouble reported there, but he pointed out that the road between Zinder and Agades was mined.

'I know someone in Zinder who might be able to help,' Liman suggested, as he tapped a number into his mobile.

'C'est Liman,' he announced into the phone. 'I have un client who's thinking of travelling between Zinder and Nguigmi. Can you help?' There was a pause – and he replaced the mobile on the table.

'What happened?' I asked.

'He said,' Liman replied with a confused grin, 'that it was too dangerous and he didn't want to know anything about it. Then he hung up.'

I smiled and thanked him for his advice, whereupon he enquired if I needed a lift into Niamey.

'He didn't want to know,' Liman repeated, as if bewildered, still struggling to make sense of it. 'He didn't want to know.'

After negotiating a potholed road past squalid buildings, scummy kerbs and a meandering rubbish dump that seemed to be an informal marker of the city's periphery, we drove along a leafy avenue that was bordered by the vast defensive gates of the American Embassy on one side and the Presidential Palace's fortress-like boundary walls on the other.

'That is,' Liman said, peering into the pothole in front of us as his face rumpled with concern, 'exactly the type of place where *they* plant the mines.'

I was not quite sure which '*they*' he was referring to, but I nodded in polite agreement as he steered around the subject of his concern; and, in truth, I had not planned on making a risk assessment on every pothole I saw. Nonetheless I marked it and can still see the depth of the hollow: its shape, form, colour, contours and size – indeed every frayed and shaded detail in relation to its composition, situation in the road and connection to its surroundings.

3

As I stepped into the vast lobby, a soldier turned towards me. He was dressed in field camouflage, a green beret and calf-high army boots, and a pistol was strapped into his holster. Beneath his look of resigned indifference, I sensed a hidden petulance.

'I am here,' I said, 'to see the Director of Tourism.'

After receiving laconic directions, I walked across the echoing space towards the stairs, noticing the different kinds of clothing worn by the people wandering past or quietly conversing. A minority, dressed in vivid robes and turbans, appeared to glide across the marble-looking floor, while others, in suits or jackets, seemed to belong to different racial categories altogether, as though the present activity in the lobby mirrored Niger's ethnic mixture.

I climbed the stairs and walked along a corridor until I found the Director's office. Outside the door was a small anteroom where two women in bright floral dresses, their hair buried beneath bundled scarves, waited in front of a woman sitting at a bureau. I explained to her that I had been given an introduction to the Director. A few minutes later Ibrahim emerged and, after some words with the secretary, invited me into a large room overlooking Niamey. He slipped into a revolving, black leather seat, and I perched on one of two chairs in front of his desk, which was adorned with a little flag of Niger, a photograph of the president, a trim pile of paper and a phone.

He studied me closely as I mentioned Akly, and explained that I had come here to discover where, if at all with the ongoing rebellion, I could travel. If I couldn't accompany a Tuareg caravan from Agades to Katsina, then I would like to journey by camel through the terrain north-east of Zinder – across the Manga. I explained I was an author, only interested in travelling with nomads through their landscape as they did and, being aware of the suspicion with which whites were perceived since the arrest of the French journalists, I stressed that I had never done any journalism – a fact that I was now most grateful for.

I turned to the plate section of my book about Inner Asia, which I had brought along for exactly this purpose, and flicked through a few photographs of migrating reindeer herders and their tepees.

'I have,' I said respectfully, 'come here to be transparent, but if you have a problem with a European travel writer being in Niger at this time, I will get on the next flight back to Britain.' There was a protracted pause as he shifted through silent deliberations towards a decision. 'I hope my French,' I continued, 'has not let me down.'

'You have explained yourself well,' Ibrahim said. 'You can stay.'

'Thank you.'

'I would like to invite one of my colleagues to join us, then we can discuss where it's possible for you to go,' he said, as he dialled a number on his desk phone.

Moments later, a lean man in his late thirties, kitted out in a burgundy suit, walked jauntily into the office. Ibrahim introduced me to Moumouni Hamadou, a fellow director. I unfolded my map and asked them to indicate which areas of the country – two-thirds of which is desert, mostly populated by nomads – were out of bounds. Moumouni traced a line along the side of a sheet of white paper that began in Zinder and went north-east to Tasker, then east to the desert settlement of Ngourti on the Chad border and south to Nguigmi. I asked him to mark the western boundaries as well, and he pencilled a stroke between Zinder and Tanout and, from there, north-west to Abalak and down to Tahoua. In short, everything north of the 16th parallel was unauthorised, which was effectively half of the country.

'You can get to Agades by military escort, but travel outside of the town is forbidden. You could always talk to the governor there,' Ibrahim suggested. 'Things change… But Agades is far from here,' he continued, as if delivering a covert warning.

Everything pointed to the Manga, the region north-east of Zinder, which I had heard about shortly before I left Agades. I recounted to the Director and Moumouni how I had visited Agades three years before, having gone there to copy Neolithic rock carvings in the Aïr. Even then, there had been an embargo on the mountains, because Rhissa ag Boula, Niger's Tourist Minister and a rebel leader during the first Tuareg rebellion, had been imprisoned in Niamey on an alleged murder charge, and his brother, Mohammed, had kidnapped some soldiers in return for his release. The mention of ag Boula's name was enough to provoke a reaction from the company I was in. 'You are always here at these times,' Moumouni commented, a quizzical gleam in his eye.

'It's not my fault,' I said with a smile, hoping to avoid being tarnished by any further suspicion.

Both Moumouni and Ibrahim insisted that the Ministry must approve my route and that I had to travel with a guide. The Manga, the area I was being given permission to travel across, was home to the Tubu. They were a people I knew next to nothing about, except that they lived in the desert, wore robes and turbans, and fought against the government in the first Tuareg rebellion. Céline had once described them to me as: 'the toughest of all Niger's nomads'. And I felt a sense of excitement about venturing into this little-known nomadic terrain that had somehow been mislaid by the modern world. Moumouni volunteered to give me a couple of Tubu contacts who might be able to help and, after thanking Ibrahim, we left his office and he went off to find the details. I waited, slightly away from the lively throng, which clustered on the landing next to the stairs, and noticed that some men had collected around a wiry, middle-aged Tuareg in an eggshell-blue robe and white turban.

'How is it in Agades?' someone enquired.

'*Les mines!*' he replied jocularly, as if trying to defuse the question. '*Les mines!*'

On his return Moumouni introduced me to the blue-robed Tuareg who was, I learnt, just passing through Niamey.

'I think I've seen you before,' he said quietly.

'Perhaps you have,' I replied. 'I spent a couple of months in Agades three years ago.' As I gazed into his hazy umber irises, deep-set in wrinkled fissures, it was as if he was searching for me in the Saharan town's twisting alleys or in the market's warren-like corridors of stalls, where repellent smells of warm meat on the cusp of rancidity mingled with the enigmatic waft of spices amid the hum of whirring sewing machines. He seemed unable to find an anchorage for me in his memory and, as our conversation became lost in questions about Agades from other voices, I felt him still examining me from the corner of his eye.

Moumouni then scratched down the mobile number of Omar Souleymane, a Tubu based in Nguigmi whom he knew to be briefly in Niamey. I descended the stairs into the lobby and walked out into the sunlight. I climbed into the front seat of the battered taxi, and the driver, Harouma, twisted the ignition key and reversed out of the courtyard into Niamey's bustling heart. Even though it was a temperate 70°F, many people were wrapped up in coats and had brightly coloured woolly hats tugged down over their ears. Harouma, like most of those who live in Niamey, was Djerma: an ethnicity that comprises almost a quarter of Niger's population. The Djerma are a people of westernmost Niger and their dialect is a branch of the Nilo-Saharan language family.

As we drove into calmer streets on the way back to the hotel, the road became empty except for a car meandering along in front of us. It was crammed with people sitting on top of each other; their torsos and heads moulded at odd angles into the cramped space. As I watched a man on the side of the road leading two camels laden with reed mats, an explosion shattered the atmosphere. Harouma's body flexed and his face buckled with anxiety.

'It's all right,' I said, as a cloud of reddish dust burst under the vehicle in front, 'it's only a tyre.'

'The Americans here,' Harouma explained, as we drove past the US embassy, 'are afraid since the explosion last week.'

'What do people think about them?' I enquired.

'They don't care about us.'

'And the French?'

'They look down on us,' he replied with a look of suppressed irritation. 'They are rude, as they were when Niger was theirs.'

'And the government?'

'No one cares.'

'I hope that will change one day.'

'*Insha'allāh.*'

4

Omar Souleymane arrived at *Les Roniers* dressed in a yellow robe and white turban, which looked less well groomed than the Tuareg fashion, but there was order in the knotted disarray: the thick pleat that coiled around his head, the tail that sagged over the right side of his chest, and the band twisted under his jaw. His turban was both an indication of a distinctive people and a mark of his individuality. Nor did he possess the naturally haughty disposition of the Tuaregs. His ebony-tinged, middle-aged face was rotund, even cherubic, and he had a wiry beard.

Omar's spoken French was monosyllabic, although I sensed he understood much of what was said. He was accompanied by two other Tubu, one of whom, Chele, a lean man in his late twenties wearing dark glasses, acted as translator. After introductions, we gathered around a wrought iron table, as shadowy hues crept across the veranda to the sound of awakening cicadas, and I explained my plans for crossing the Manga by camel. We all peered at the map and then Chele circled a settlement to the north-east of Zinder: Birnin Kazoe.

'Many nomads go to the market there to sell their camels,' Chele said. Omar then spoke in Tubu.

'He says,' Chele explained, 'that we should buy the camels in Nguigmi because they are cheaper, wait for a caravan and then travel with them north-west.' Omar's finger trailed over the Manga along the fringe between the Sahara and the Sahel towards the Termit Mountains and, from there, south to Birnin Kazoe, 'where,' Chele observed, 'you can sell the camels at the end of your trip.' At a glance it looked like a journey of about six hundred kilometres as the crow flies.

'How long will it take?' I asked.

'*Un mois*,' Omar replied, before slipping back into Tubu.

'Omar suggests,' Chele translated, 'that he will be your guide and, because you need a translator as well, you will have to buy three camels.'

When I explained that we had to get our month-long route agreed by the authorities, they both looked surprised.

'Because of the rebellion,' I persisted. 'We cannot go without permits. It's what I've been told by the Ministry of Tourism's Director.'

'Of course,' Chele conceded. 'We will meet at the Ministry tomorrow morning.'

I escorted them to the front of the hotel, where the azan floated across the dusky sky from somewhere beyond the boundaries of *Les Roniers*: '*Allāhu Akbar… Allāhu Akbar.*' The chant paused, and there came a fading chorus of bird song, as the evening star glittered; then the consoling summons to prayer continued through the slumbering twilight: '*Allāhu Akbar… Allāhu Akbar.*'

*   *   *

As the shadows of bats zipped through the lucent night, I became aware that Annie Colas had stepped out of the restaurant and was sauntering towards me.

'It's a good thing you're going to do,' she said, as if dispelling any doubts I had about travelling through an unknown region in a country gripped by rebellion. 'Pierre has told me about your journey with the Tubu.'

'Thanks for that,' I answered, genuinely pleased to hear her say it.

'I have never been where you are going, but I have travelled with the Wodaabe,' she said reflectively.

The Wodaabe, or Bororo, are a branch of West Africa's Fulani people – the world's largest nomadic group, whose origins are somewhat disputed. The French refer to the Fulani as the Peul. The Wodaabe speak Fulfulde, a soft, melodious language, and they don't use the written word. They have no concept of God: they call the sky '*Allah*.' Nor do they have a word for 'government' – as with 'God' they recognise it only as recognised by others. Migrating through the Sahel with their herds of zebu, a breed of long-horned cattle with drooping ears and a hefty dewlap, the Wodaabe inhabit a semiarid world where the sandy ground is a thorny mat of spiky burs, nail-like thorns, scorched rocks and petrified fragments.

The Wodaabe are renowned for their beauty, elaborate garments and colourful ceremonies. They are, in short, aesthetes. As Annie talked of the Wodaabe, I remembered my time with them: their rhythmic, tidal chanting, the wafting aroma of campfires and the sharp odour of body sweat as they swayed in unison, like the pulse of an ocean swell.

As a bat skimmed across the pool's silky surface, Annie described how a pair of storks returned each year to nest in the baobab, and that over sixty-five different species of birds made their home – at some point during the year – at *Les Roniers*. She pointed to a tree, the size of a mature oak, which looked as if it belonged in the jungle and explained that it was called a *caoutchouc*. Its muscular trunk, furrowed with deep grooves and gullies, supported a flourishing canopy that draped and rambled above the pool, and magnolia-like leaves periodically curled through the void before landing gracefully on the water. 'It was in a pot in the restaurant,' Annie continued, 'but it wasn't doing very well. I transplanted it fifteen years ago... and now look at it.'

'Amazing,' I replied.

'The American ambassador,' she recounted, 'once observed on a visit here how the grounds of the embassy were almost completely devoid of bird-song in contrast to *Les Roniers*. I pointed out that it might be something to do with the fact that the trees planted in his grounds weren't indigenous.'

Annie's family roots were in Provence, but she was brought up on the Ivory Coast with her four siblings, her parents having moved there in 1925. She met her husband, who grew up in

Chénas, on a family holiday to Beaujolais, and they had lived in Niamey for twenty-eight years. Together she and Pierre ran the hotel and its staff, most of who seemed to be related to one another. Pierre had the quintessential look of a French café owner, with a paunch and a gravelly voice that sometimes slipped into a growl, and he enjoyed his cigarettes and small glasses of red Burgundy.

*   *   *

The next morning, permission was secured for our journey across the Manga. My ministry permit read: *Moyen de Transport – Méharée Cameline.* Omar and I agreed to meet in Nguigmi the following Friday. It is approximately one thousand five hundred kilometres from Niamey to Nguigmi, a bus journey from one side of the country to the other, which is completed in two stages, Zinder being half-way. I had somehow contracted a pugnacious bowel ailment; the last thing I needed in the wilderness was a debilitating virus, so Harouma drove me to the Gamkalley clinic for a diagnosis.

The dusty, reddish road that led to the clinic wound alongside the Niger, where a few people, naked apart from loincloths, were washing their laundry, and a couple of sinewy young men, their skin glistening in the sun, trawled nets through the swirling pools dotted among the riverbank's quivering reeds. The clinic was perched on a ridge slightly back from the river and its charges were beyond the pockets of most citizens. Dr Jean Daniel Yovanovitch, in his late thirties and living in Niamey with his wife and two children, supervised the private facility. He ambled toward me with his hands snugly content in the pockets of his white coat and a stethoscope hung around his neck.

I followed the doctor along a spotlessly clean corridor to his office and he invited me to sit down. I explained that I had diarrhoea, a slight fever, had been taking ciprofloxacin and usually would not have bothered to seek medical advice, but, because I was heading into the wilderness for a month, thought it wiser to do so.

'Be careful how much ciproflox you take,' he advised. 'It weakens the tendons.'

'Okay,' I concurred, nodding meekly.

'You should be all right where you are going,' Jean Daniel observed, as the chilly disc of his stethoscope pressed against my chest. 'It's still reasonably safe, but you should know that all expats are avoiding Agades at the moment.'

'So I've been warned.'

'I'd like to take a blood sample,' he proposed. 'I think you've caught a virus that's going around, but I don't think you've been here long enough to have malaria. Are you taking tablets?'

'Malarone.'

'They're the best,' he acknowledged, 'but none of them are completely foolproof.'

'What does the French community in Niamey,' I probed, diverging from the subject of my anatomical workings, 'think about the imprisoned journalists?'

'There was,' he said, 'something in the paper that ran: "*The French Community Mobilises*",' he paused for effect. '*Full stop*,' he added, stressing the punctuation mark. 'And that was it. Most people are unsympathetic. They were irresponsible and have compromised us all.' He dabbed some methylated spirit onto a ball of cotton wool, held my forearm and injected a syringe into a braided blue vein, and I watched the cylindrical tube fill up with dark, viscous liquid. 'I really wouldn't want to be in their place,' he observed. 'That prison they're in; it's rotten, seriously rotten.' I tried not to imagine the horrors of languishing in a West African prison. 'Now,' he pondered, removing the needle. 'What would I want to take with me for a long trip into the bush?'

5

The two journalists were released the day after AREVA, the French nuclear group, and the Niger government struck a mega-deal in Niamey, or so I read in some local rag called *Le Témoin*. France is the world's second largest producer of atomic energy, and Niger's Aïr Mountains are home to one of the world's foremost uranium deposits; the two nations, it appeared, had a gilded, but prickly relationship. The reporters were driven from their cells directly to the airport and put on a plane bound for Paris; their local driver and guide, however, were not as fortunate and remained incarcerated as a warning not requiring any public explanation. For the next twenty-four hours *Les Roniers'* television was saturated with coverage of the release, and then the two French journalists disappeared from the screen and became part of the past. For the first time since my arrival eight days earlier, Niger – ranked by the World Bank as the planet's poorest country, with virtually two-thirds of its fifteen million population earning less than $1 a day – was not world news material and, despite the recent explosion in the city and the rebellion's imminent first anniversary, I sensed a cautious mellowing in Niamey's atmosphere.

I sat on the bed in my room flicking through *Paris Match*, and came across an article about a French anthropologist who lived with an Amazonian tribe. These people governed their lives with a philosophy of sharing and moderation: a concept that seemed in stark contrast to the hundred square metres that were felled every second in their jungle, as the article explained. Distracted by a skittering, I glanced up. A murky-green lizard scampered along a wall and into the air vent; its skimpy tail flickering briefly, as if pausing for balance, before it vanished into one of the vent's dark slits.

Through the open doorway, I watched hotel staff go about their chores; a hosepipe snaked across the sienna-coloured ground, and the air was filled with the aroma of fresh water on steamy vegetation. The dishevelled blue backpack sat all hunched up on a chair depleted of its contents, which were carefully laid out on the spare bed. Only a couple of weeks previously, when I had extracted it from the garage, my pack had been in such a state of retirement that I discovered a mouse had made a nest in the bottom of it. Now I had to decide what to take into the Manga, with every object having to fight for its place.

I had forgotten to bring my French–English dictionary and shampoo; in addition I needed a tube of toothpaste, a metal mug, matches, two plastic containers with lids, a tyre repair kit for my inflatable mattress and a towel. I called Harouma on his mobile and, half an hour later, he arrived for an excursion to the market: a rambling island of stalls bubbling with activity in the city centre opposite the police headquarters.

It was difficult, as we drove along the rutted roads, to ignore the disease and disfigurement that haunted the city's nucleus. Nearly every traffic light harboured lingering beggars, whose faces and bodies were marked with affliction: hepatic-yellow eyes; distended cheeks; hollow gazes that had long lost the strength to glower; febrile shivers; gaunt forms that huddled in squalid, crusty rags; finger stumps mangled by leprosy; bloated skin disorders; and ghoulish, cloudy-white irises that seemed to have had the life frozen out of them. These human beings – besieged by sickness – existed in a desperate state of constant, gnawing deterioration. They seemed mostly ignored by the surrounding whirl of daily activity, as if they did not exist, and blind people shuffled through the chalky-russet dust with cupped palms.

These days, the urban beggars have to compete for attention with the mobile phone, a phenomenon that did not exist in Niger three years previously. We saw clutches of teenagers in stained jeans and T-shirts scramble towards cars waiting at the lights to thrust pay-as-you-go scratch cards through the windows. It was with silent relief that we pulled away from all this commotion, and headed for the market. Harouma parked in a busy, narrow lane, just wide enough for another car to pass and, stepping onto the grimy road, we left the calm confines of his vehicle.

The market place was fizzing with 'busyness', as if it was a living organism in its own right. Alleyways of stalls spun off in opposing directions and there was a constant stream of chatter – sometimes punctuated with isolated pockets of frenetic dialogue or fragmentary ululations – as people wandered through the cramped and twisting lanes of cubicles. And we wound our way past stalls of hacked goat joints smothered with flies, tables stacked with vegetables and bundles of trussed up chickens that lay gasping in the dust.

*   *   *

In the dark hours of the following morning, with the sky scintillating with stars, I watched my pack disappear into the bus's luggage hold and, carrying my knapsack, I climbed onto the curtained bus and settled into a seat at the back. A short while later, the bus shuddered to the command of a grumbling engine, and we rumbled along empty streets and past the hushed market, as the city was slowly gobbled up into the blackness by the shadows and silhouettes of impoverished suburbs. Finally, they too were dissolved into the ghostly forms of a landscape without end, as we headed east towards Zinder.

6

It took fourteen hours to get to the old French colonial capital of Zinder, the road deteriorating by degrees till I felt my sacroiliac joint dislodge itself. After a deplorable night's sleep, I abandoned the sordid hotel I had booked into and decamped to the *Amadou Kouran Daga* outside the town centre, situated in its own private compound. It boasted a large courtyard, where the few guests could park their cars, and flimsy acacias provided a gauzy scattering of shade. The rooms were clean and capacious; mine even had a bath that supplied a dash of hot water. On the balcony outside the hotel's Soviet-style restaurant, five vibrantly woven carpets were spread out, as if each were a shop, on which camel-hide ornaments, daggers, swords, Neolithic arrowheads, saddlebags and Tuareg jewellery were meticulously arrayed. And two Tuaregs in black robes and turbans, their faces hidden apart from their eyes and the jutting bridge of their noses, huddled in the courtyard sand, making thimbles of tea over a nest of embers.

I had arranged with Ilyia, a slender young man wearing dark glasses and a red baseball cap, to take me to the sultan's palace – we had met when he ferried me between hotels. As he didn't speak French, we communicated with a pen and paper or I pointed to the hands of his watch. I clambered onto the moped behind him, he engaged the accelerator and we sped past some bikers lingering outside the hotel gates, and onto the main road that led into the town centre. As we wove between the traffic and the potholes, leaving a plume of dust behind us, there was a certain sense of cultural integration.

We pulled up under the palace's formidable sepia walls, where two barefoot guards dressed in emerald and carmine robes stood either side of the entrance, the rugged contours of each ebony face framed in the sleek coils of a scarlet turban. A man in a white robe and pot-like Hausa hat emerged from the gateway's arched shadows and, scurrying towards us, introduced himself as one of the guardians – his eyelids twitching in time with his rapidly spoken French. He offered to show me around and I gestured to Ilyia to come too. My pupils dilated as we followed our guide into the narrow, dimly lit entrance while he recounted, with obvious pride, that the sultan had over two hundred bodyguards.

We stepped back out into the glare and found ourselves in a square, sandy courtyard dotted with a few small metallic doors. These had once led, our guide indicated, to cells where wretched prisoners were locked up, with ants or scorpions, for twenty-four hours at a time depending on their crime; it sounded more like a sadistic death sentence. At his insistence, I peered into one of the miserably cramped closets that had just enough space for a man to take three steps. It was not difficult to visualise the horror of spending a minute, let alone any protracted period, in the dark cavity crawling with venomous arachnids. As we walked across the courtyard, we learnt the surrounding mud walls contained the bones of the sultan's enemies, put there when the palace was built two centuries ago.

I removed my shoes and carried their heels in the crook of two fingers of my right hand, as we stepped through a doorway leading into the palace interior. By European standards, there was nothing palatial about the building or its rooms; it was, both in appearance and architecture, more like a Saharan fort. We walked along a simple corridor, empty of furniture, towards a low doorway.

'The Sultan of Zinder,' our guide announced reverentially, 'is in the next room, holding an audience with the Youth Minister.' We followed him through the open door and found ourselves among an elite group waiting in a diminutive courtyard outside the audience chamber's grandiose doors, which were guarded by a brawny policeman armed with a machine gun and a pistol.

The elegantly attired gathering of both sexes looked vaguely surprised to see us, as we settled ourselves discreetly at the back. Our guide's narration diminished to a whisper and his sentences began to gallop as he explained how the littered, sandy alley immediately behind us was where prisoners used to receive judgment and, if found guilty, were to be executed in the dimly lit space beyond the cavernous doorway at its end.

Amid the sounds of muted conversations around us, I became aware that the person standing beside me was listening to us: a bald, muscular, well-built man with liquorice-coloured skin. At a pause in the narrative, he introduced himself as Djbrilla Namalka, explaining that he was a journalist who had travelled from Niamey to cover the meeting between the sultan and the minister.

'I am also captain of Niger's rugby team,' he continued in confident French. 'Unlike European professionals, my colleagues and I have to supplement our passion with an alternative job.'

'What position do you play?' I enquired, warming to his resilient demeanour.

'Mostly, the second row,' he replied, sliding a pair of sunglasses up onto his gleaming brow. 'My team is joint champion of Africa's second division, but we have no financial support. There was an American who worked for the World Bank and lived in Niamey for a while; he gave us $5,000 a year, but he's left and we have no patron. The government allocates just $90,000 a year for all of Niger's sporting endeavours.'

'Do you think you could beat any of the European teams?'

'We would hold our own,' he answered decisively. 'We'd love to have that opportunity.'

Djbrilla explained that he also worked as a TV presenter and knew the journalist who had been killed by the mine in Niamey; he had been with him at a social gathering just a few hours before the explosion. As he described this, his eyes suggested a momentary vulnerability, but then the doors to the audience chamber swung open and silence settled over those assembled there. A voluptuous middle-aged woman, clad in a black tunic-like dress, and an ageing man were slowly emerging through the doorway.

An official indicated to Djbrilla that this was the time for him to take his photographs, and he threaded his way towards the sixty-year-old sultan, the minister and her bodyguard, who were slowly filing past. Like a wedding congregation, the rest of us tagged on and we followed them back into the central courtyard, where the throng loosely collected around another official who began to give a speech. Our guide, taking the opportunity to show us a room that was not usually accessible to the public, led us back to the impressively large audience chamber. At the far end was a huge throne-like sofa and, backed up against the walls around the room, there were smaller sofas, as if to suggest a seating hierarchy. Large, framed photographs of dignitaries lined the walls; one of whom I recognised as the Sultan of Agades, Ibrahim Umaru, from when I had met him at his home. I peered, once again, past those furrows into his sooty eyes where iris and pupil became one. It had been three years since the sultan gestured to me, with an elegant shuffle of his right arm, to sit down on the chair beside him. Knowing that he had visited Europe and America, I asked whether he preferred New York or London.

'I have been to New York, Washington and Chicago,' the willowy sultan had replied with a husky softness, and there arose a flicker of nostalgic happiness tapped from memories beyond the desert.

'What did you think of Lake Michigan?' The flicker became a glow and, for a moment that belonged outside time, weary wrinkles were obliterated as a smile banished tiresome anxieties, and we talked about the dinosaurs exhibited in Washington. Palaeontology led on to London and I listened as he relived Piccadilly, and climbed the stairs of Tower Bridge, from where I sensed him gazing over London's endless glistening panorama of buildings and roads.

'Where did you stay?' I asked, searching for further common ground.

The sultan descended from Tower Bridge and the panorama vanished, illusory as a mirage.

'I stayed in a private home,' he replied, tendering nothing further. Whether he interpreted my question as a probe or, in his answer, he had been taken to a more mundane space; the embers evaporated, the spark was extinguished, the gaunt wrinkles returned and the happy memories vanished beneath a mask. At the time of this conversation, as in the formal portrait on the wall, the sultan was dressed in a pristine white robe and turban, and I briefly wondered how he was doing at his palace beneath the mosque's imposing minaret, and how the rebellion might be affecting him.

Ilyia, the guide and I left the carpeted chamber and walked back to the courtyard where the twenty-third Sultan of Zinder was escorting the minister through the main entrance. After her black, chauffeur-driven Mercedes slid out of view beyond the framed archway, the sultan hobbled back towards the door that led to the private rooms where he lived with his three wives and some of his twenty-three children. He wore a Hausa hat and emerald robes, and used his majestic silver staff more as a walking prop than for any ceremonial function.

'What's the matter with him?' I asked discreetly.

'He has,' the guide explained, 'sickness in his feet.'

I did not push for a more distinct diagnosis, but watched his painful progress across the dust as a troop of colourfully dressed bodyguards jumped around him in ritual ceremony, whooping loudly as they did so. There was a quiet dignity in his limping gait. After he, and his entourage, disappeared into the shadows of a doorway, the chanting seemed to hum for an instant above the deserted courtyard, as if the chorus was contemplating its own evanescence, and then all was silent except for the rustle of a small plastic bag that was scooped into the air by an unruly breeze.

*   *   *

The town's old quarter is situated behind the sultan's palace, and is made up of a network of meandering lanes polluted by litter and black puddles. Many of the mud dwellings bordering the lanes were stencilled with the decorative markings of Hausa architecture, and I peered into the ruins of the house where, between 25 December 1852 and 30 January 1853, had stayed Henry Barth, the German explorer appointed by the British Government to travel into Central Africa and report on the abolition of slaves. Barth's room in Agades, at *La Maison D'Annur*, which he used for three weeks in October 1850 on his way to Kano, has survived, and retains his bed, camel saddles and travelling chests in a space redolent of a man in transit, as if he could walk in at any moment. Nothing remains though, of his guest quarters in Zinder, except some crumbling walls and a corroding plaque in French testifying to his stay there.

Barth wrote of his stay in Zinder:

> Being most anxious to complete my scientific labours and researches in regard to Bornu, and send home as much of my journal as possible in order not to expose it to any risk, I stayed most of the time in my quarters, which I had comfortably fitted up with a good supply of 'siggedi' or coarse reed mats, taking only now and then, in the afternoon, a ride on horseback.

On his extraordinary five-year expedition, Henry Barth became the first European to penetrate Agades officially. He often travelled along the Sahara's old caravan routes that, on the map, look like an untidy cobweb spun across the hostile wastelands from Marrakech to Timbuktu; Tripoli to Lake Chad; Fez to Cairo, and Constantine to the southern entrepots of Agades, Zinder, Kano and Katsina. These ancient tracks were the arteries of commerce and pilgrimage, linking the Gulf of Guinea to the Mediterranean and the Atlantic to the Red Sea. Barth continued: 'Besides some indigo-dyeing, there is scarcely any industry in Zinder; yet its commercial importance has of late become so great, that it may with some propriety be called "The gate of Sudan".'

I left the dilapidated remnants of the space that was once home to Henry Barth in an unknown land and wandered along an alley past a smiling man with a streaky-white goatee, who wore a snowy Hausa hat and an inky-green robe. He sat on a reed mat, comfortably hunched up against the open entrance to his home, his fingers caressing a necklace of Qur'anic beads; and his baby granddaughter, naked apart from a woolly hat and red jersey, sat beside him studying me in the afternoon's glimmering light.

7

Unknown to me, on the day I arrived in Zinder, MNJ Tuareg rebels attacked the small town of Tanout, situated a hundred kilometres to the north, on the road to Agades. The BBC felt it sufficiently noteworthy to warrant a bulletin. 'The rebels,' they announced on their website, 'say they abducted eleven people, including the mayor, from Tanout, nine hundred kilometres north-east of Niamey.' The MNJ, I later learned, had a website and a blog. I had been warned, at the Ministry of Tourism in Niamey, that the provinces were, in many ways, a law unto themselves, and permissions granted in the capital were not necessarily absolute; they advised that, on arrival at any provincial seat, it would be prudent to check in with the authorities. With their counsel in mind, but at that point unaware of the rebel incursion just up the road, I asked Ilyia to take me to where I could find Zinder's regional governor. We sped off on his moped through the commotion of the town centre. After pausing at a set of traffic lights where a ragged woman, racked by crazy, frenzied laughter, sat scrabbling in the dust, we scooted along quiet streets that filtered towards the town's airy suburbs.

Ilyia stopped outside a low-level complex of municipal buildings and I noticed, in the immediate surroundings, a scattered presence of soldiers dressed in desert khaki with burgundy berets – all equipped with semi-automatics. I walked down a flagstone path to some open glass doors, where an armed policeman stood alertly in the centre of an oval foyer; the atmosphere was electric, as if charged with sense-sharpening adrenalin. Even the acoustic seemed to have been heightened, despite the quiet, controlled dialogue that drifted out of open doorways. A guard pointed out where I could find the governor's secretary, and I walked over to the office he indicated.

Three men, dressed in smart Western clothing, were loosely huddled around a desk in earnest, but calm conversation. I introduced myself to the person whom I took to be the governor's secretary, and explained about my trip with the Tubu. Unfolding the permission I'd been granted in Niamey, I clarified that I had come to see the governor just to check in, as I would be travelling through his patch. We then progressed to the half-open door of another room, spacious and well lit, and found a middle-aged man dressed in a chestnut leather jacket, a black shirt and a pair of trim dark trousers. He was engaged in a conversation on his landline and stood slightly to one side of the bureau; as we waited, the phone cord gently tugged his wrist, as if prompting him not to stray from its orbit.

He looked preoccupied and distracted when he put the phone down, and from the couple of fleeting glances he slid in my direction I sensed that I was the last thing he needed. His secretary briefly recounted what I had told him.

'I am the governor,' he announced, 'Yahaya Yandaka.'

'I have been granted authorisation,' I said, handing him my permit, 'by the Ministry of Tourism, to travel with the Tubu. This journey takes me across your *département* and I wanted to see you, bearing in mind the troubles around Agades and the suspicion in which white people are currently held, just as a matter of transparency and courtesy.'

I had no idea, when I stepped into the building, that there was any prospect of my trip being jeopardised, so was surprised to hear the governor retort in a tone that bordered on a growl:

'You may have authorisation from Niamey, but you will need permission from *le Chef de Tourisme* in Zinder. It is with him that this decision now lies.' He picked up the phone. '*J'ai un blanc ici,*' he sighed dismissively and, after a brief explanation, hung up. 'How did you travel here today?'

'By moped,' I answered.

'You're in luck,' he mused, and I felt a marginal shift in his attitude towards me, though that might have been because, at least for the moment, I was no longer his problem. '*Le Chef de Tourisme* is called Omarou Arzika. He is around, and I've just spoken to his assistant. I will come outside and give your driver instructions on how to get there.'

We walked back across the foyer. As we stepped outside, two formidable armed soldiers emerged on our flanks and escorted us to Ilyia where, in the brooding shadow of their Rottweiler-like presence, the governor issued directions. I thanked him. As we zipped up the driveway, I was aware of the governor monitoring us, until a trio of officials emerged, and he pivoted towards the building amid what seemed like a swirl of dispatches.

The Tourism office was conveniently based close to the hotel, and I asked Ilyia to wait in its gated forecourt. I skipped up the few steps into a building that, at a glance, could quite easily have been converted into a pleasant home, and stepped into the shady reception hall. From there, I walked through the only open doorway, along a short corridor into a room where a lean man was dictating a letter.

'*Le Chef de Tourisme?*' I enquired.

'Come into my office,' he answered. Shafts of light illuminated the small adjoining room, and one of the walls was covered with a map of the *département* of Zinder. I sat down facing him across the cluttered table.

'You do know,' he continued, getting up and fingering the map, 'that rebels attacked Tanout on Monday?'

'No,' I replied, sensing my trip was in danger of being vetoed. 'I didn't.'

'They killed three people and kidnapped the town prefect.'

'Look,' I said, understanding at last, 'here is my permit issued by the Ministry in Niamey. The only reason I checked in with the governor was to be transparent. I have no agenda. All I want to do is to travel with the Tubu just as they do across their landscape.'

'Where you want to go is north of where this last raid occurred,' he observed.

'Most people in Britain don't even know that Niger exists,' I replied, quickly grasping for a solution. 'At best, they confuse it with Nigeria.' I watched his expression transform from creased severity into the softer contours of understanding, as he recognised the truth in my last sentence. 'As a travel writer,' I persisted, 'I might be able to help. You have a great country with wonderful people.'

'*Alors*,' he said, after silently tussling with the conundrum, 'you may proceed, but I want to take five photocopies of your permit for circulation to the region's authorities.' I handed him my permit. He pressed a seal into a sponge of Prussian blue ink and stamped the crumpled sheet of paper at the bottom. He then initialled it and wrote in biro: *Visa arrivée à Zinder 24/1/2008.*

'You must,' he insisted, 'report back here on your return.' After asking his secretary to photocopy the permit he returned the original. '*Bonne route.*'

'*Merci*,' I replied, and stepped out of his office and back into the afternoon sunlight.

*   *   *

Zinder's market had an altogether different character from the one in Niamey. Discreetly tucked away behind what appeared to be a rambling colonial building, which stretched along a bustling street, it impressed the visitor as a separate entity in its own right, with different rules and regulations. It had a timeless atmosphere that might have belonged to any century within the last two thousand years. The alleys between the stalls were more like lanes and, walking though them, it felt like being in the current of a brook. There was a sensation of unwritten order in the sprawling market's physical and social anatomy, as people glided or strolled through the maze of stalls; the atmosphere was free of any agitation – of voice or gesture – and there was no jostling.

Stalls displayed green oranges, dwarf melons, disfigured cucumbers, dates, gnarled vegetable roots, lettuces, tomatoes and tubs of vibrantly-coloured spices, all competing with one another. Then, on the turn of a corner, was a network of booths displaying long rolls of brightly-coloured textiles. Another segment of the market was allocated to shoes; another reserved for decoratively bundled Sahelian grasses; one corner was heavy with the drone of flies clustering round some tables arranged with ugly chunks of greying meat; and at the back was a space reserved for the sale of sugar cane, where children giggled contentedly as they sucked on the dark, sweet sticks. Beside them was a section in which second-hand tyres were set out, its position on the market's periphery suggesting that it marked the separation of old from new. The Grand Market then curled back in on itself into rows of stores selling household goods, with shelves of neatly piled tins of sardines and tuna, cans of spam and corned beef, packets of biscuits, sweets, pasta, matches, sugar and a generous display of toiletries; after which the stalls shifted into another category, and another, while the Nigériens moved through the config-uration of alleys like corpuscles in a network of capillaries. The air was a marinade of smells that blended and shunted into one another as they tickled, appeased or affronted the olfactory nerves.

8

Zinder dissolved into the blackness. An eighteen-hour journey lay ahead of us. As we travelled east to Nguigmi, on the Chad border, I wrapped a blanket around me and tucked my chin into a tight pleat. The shuddering bus looked as if it had been languishing in some long-abandoned quarry: half of the windows were missing while the other half were threaded with spidery patterns, like hoar frost puddles, and the torn, foam-padded seats were mostly separated from their tiny metal frames. The floor was piled with canvas sacks and containers, and passengers hunched beside one another cocooned in blankets. The frigid night, the acrid stench of diesel, the engine's rumbling cacophony and the rolling motion induced the sense of being at sea on some decrepit fishing trawler.

The stars began to lose their sparkle, and slowly fade into the colours of dawn. On the roof, above us, there was a tower of luggage, sacks and jerry cans – all fastidiously fastened down with ropes. The windows were scratched with a web of grime-encrusted cracks and, as the sun pulled out of sight above us, our cabin was increasingly engulfed in dust, swirling as if caught in a vortex. I had forgotten the quiet sense of solidarity that settles over passengers on such a journey, and I noticed the doors were bolted from the inside, not only to keep the doors securely fastened but, seemingly, to prevent unwelcome or hostile individuals from boarding the bus.

We travelled east through the sandy Sahelian terrain, peppered with copses of palms. Date groves gradually disappeared. The landscape became increasingly bare; the only thing separating it from the desert was a thin mesh of vegetation that looked as if were woven into the ground between us and the horizon. And the dishevelled villages we travelled through were each cordoned off, at beginning and end, with rickety military checkpoints where our driver had to disembark in search of permission to proceed.

There were a few desert-people – robed and turbaned – amongst the thirty-odd passengers, but most were Hausa. The Hausa women wore vibrant dresses with scarves swaddled around their heads and the men, with pot-like hats perched on their crowns, wore knee-length shirts and cotton trousers. In contrast to the wobbling anatomies of the Hausa women, the men were lean. Some of these women babbled in loud, shrill voices, seemingly oblivious to anyone's space but their own, yet the men were silent and rarely moved. This behaviour, though, seemed to be confined to the affluent middle-aged women, as if a lady's wealth and status could be approximately measured by her girth. The two or three elderly Hausa ladies on the other hand, were discreet and modest, and the wrinkled lady sitting opposite me reached into a paper bag and offered me a pygmy banana.

The sun crept over us in a slow arc until the sky adopted the tints of a late Saharan afternoon, and then we arrived at the outskirts of Diffa, where the Hausa disembarked; the roof ropes were unravelled and belongings were disentangled from the vast mound of luggage. Outside, amid the clamour and vociferations, passengers sorted out their possessions and the bus began to assume a different vibe as a number of robed Tubu came up the steps. They seemed to float, and they settled into their seats like butterflies alighting on buddleia. Soon, veiled faces and the glint of curious pupils surrounded me.

The bus shunted forward once more and we peeled away from the rumpus, as we began the hundred-and-fifty-kilometre journey north to Nguigmi. It would take over eight hours, since the road quickly evaporated into a braided network of sandy tracks. The engine groaned and wheezed to the demand of an impatient clutch, and we tilted from side to side, as if in a swell. The ground's rippling undulations began to dissolve in the creeping hues of an early dusk. Then the bus juddered to a halt and, under a flickering evening star, the Tubu silently stepped out into the desert. After washing their hands and feet, the men stood beside one another and began the recitations of ṣalāt – the Muslim's ritual prayer – while the women formed a praying cluster of their own some distance behind.

*   *   *

As we trundled into the darkening shades, the stars emerged and the air turned chilly. The Tubu tugged their robes around their bodies and arranged their turbans tightly across their faces, as if to avoid exposing any skin. Some wrapped themselves in blankets. The crisp shades of the desert night transformed the dunes into brooding silhouettes. I became aware of glinting orange dots, winking like lighthouses, and the stink of diesel was intermittently softened by the perfume of wispy campfire smoke. The bus creaked as we lumbered and jolted slowly forward until, after a sustained chorus of mechanical shrieks, the engine gave up altogether and we were marooned in the deepening sand.

It was the beginning of a protracted series of enforced halts and, on each occasion, three men, seemingly hired for this very purpose, dug us out with shovels and steel plates peppered with rivets. The night became numbingly cold and, over the following hours, women began to disappear under blankets, looking like mounds of tarpaulin-covered luggage, and men adjusted their turbans even tighter, to restrict the freezing air exclusively to eye slits. We passed a couple of stranded lorries listing like beached container ships, while occupants struggled with the sand for their release.

*   *   *

The bus crawled through an island of campfires that seemed to denote a settlement consisting only of an alleyway of stalls. Shadows fleetingly became people, then shadows again, and the forms of robed nomads were briefly illuminated by the flickering glow of yellow flames. We heard fragments of banter punctuated with sparks and the crack of a burning branch. And then, they too, fell away and we were alone in the desert again, as stars burned in the blackness from one horizon to the other.

A Tubu boy of about thirteen sat cross-legged on the torn padded seat opposite me. He wore a purple robe and a chequered turban, with a blue veil-like garment draped over his head and fastened under his body, as if to create his own tepee, within which he could reside undisturbed; all that was visible of him were his eyes peering from behind two holes furrowed into the turban's folds with his index fingers and thumbs. He did not move from that position for the ensuing four hours but, when he was not asleep, I became aware he was observing everything around him – missing nothing. At one point, fast asleep – body pivoting on his cross-legged axis – he looked like a Russian doll as he swayed in rhythm with the rolling of the bus.

'Mustapha,' a woman said with a chuckle, as we finally arrived at the outskirts of Nguigmi. I watched the boy's eyes open. His dark pupils swivelled round the bus as he swiftly made a surveillance without stirring; sleep was instantly dismissed, but he sat there motionless and silent, and with no visible response to the calling of his name. It was 2 o'clock in the morning: the journey from Zinder had taken twenty-one hours. We were on the fringes of a town at the bottom of the Old Salt Road on the border with Chad. As I sat watching the Tubu climb out into the night, it became apparent we were at an unmanned checkpoint and would not be proceeding until we had been given authorisation in the morning.

There was no mobile reception or available landline to dial the number given to me by Omar, nor did I have an address – yet nothing seemed to matter. I was tired, my back had reached a new pitch of pain and I wasn't sure why it hadn't yet broken into spasm. I yearned for sleep. I sat alone in the freezing bus huddled in a blanket trying to assess whether I could secure a flat surface for my six-foot-five frame that was not riddled with holes, jagged edges and other bumps. Then, amid a fog of confused thoughts, one of the Tubu came over to the bus – and beckoned me to follow.

I followed him the short distance to an open hut-like structure with a canvas roof, where a dozen Tubu were collected around a fire's comforting orange and purple embers, and I was shown a narrow space in the dirt between two snoring bundles. I was just pleased to be included in some human company and, as I settled down, I noticed Mustapha silently sitting beside the cinders watching me. I eased onto the reed mat, tucked my blanket around me, used my rumpled cotton handkerchief as a tiny pillow and, between the ponderous snoring on my right and the pair of horny black feet on my left, quickly fell asleep to a companionable muffled chatter and the lacy smoke of a smouldering twig.

9

'*Debout*,' someone grunted. '*Debout*.' I blinked into bleary life, as my senses concluded there wasn't any danger. '*Debout*,' the voice shouted, seemingly enjoying its power of command, and I glanced up at a gangly man prancing around the revitalised fire and yelling at the recumbent bodies, as if it was a game. It was that time before the sun's arrival, but after the stars had disappeared, and streaks of silky mist hovered over the ground. Shuffling onto my elbow, I noticed Mustapha had gone. Our surroundings were draped in a haze and, as I slowly withdrew my blanket and the cold air washed over me, I peered at the Sahelian scrub on one side and the beginnings of Nguigmi on the other.

Amid a fractured chorus of hoarse coughs and hacking, the Tubu padded though the sand, each in search of a private space. When you travel in the wilderness, that zone between waking and the completion of ablutions is sacrosanct. It is as if there was a universal law that a person respects their travelling companions' right to a moment of conscious solitude, so that body, mind and spirit can acknowledge their relationship.

*   *   *

Our bus was authorised to proceed by a couple of soldiers, the chain across the road was unhooked, and the few remaining passengers were driven the short distance into Nguigmi. The bus halted on a sandy street lined with mud houses. I stepped into the light, blinking, and monitored my backpack as it was extracted from the mound of belongings on the roof and lowered to the ground. I scanned the empty street, seemingly inhabited only by a few brindled goats, and sifted through my options in a town bereft of accommodation, where I had no contact address. As I did so, a bulky fellow in a white robe and sandals emerged out of an open doorway and approached with an enquiring expression.

The man spoke a few phrases of French and I explained my situation. He kindly offered to help find Omar, whom he thought he knew and, reaching for my pack, heaved it onto his brawny left shoulder. I allowed him to carry it, not out of any apathy, but as a precautionary measure – the three and a half hours of profound sleep had appeased my vertebrae, but the relief was still only palliative. I followed him from one house to another, but the faces that opened the doors did not belong to the one I hoped to find and, looking somewhat fretful, my sturdy companion suggested we check in with the police. Sweat trickled from his brow to his cheeks like windowpane raindrops as we strode through deserted sandy alleys, with dung beetles blundering about us.

The rather dilapidated police post lay beyond a square that harboured some kind of municipal building. As we walked into the enclosed compound, we observed three men sitting in the shade of a rickety structure, sharing a cigarette. We stepped into a dark room where a policeman, writing at a table, looked up enquiringly. As my guide explained what he knew of me, I withdrew the ministry permit, unfolded the creased sheet and handed it over.

'*Passeport*,' the official instructed, after scrutinising the permit's contents, and I fumbled in my fleece's inside pocket and extracted the burgundy booklet. His grubby thumbs and forefingers flicked through the leaves, and he pressed a seal into a sponge of scarlet ink and stamped the bottom of the page beside the Paris-issued visa. '*L'arrivée à N'guigmi 26/1/08*,' he wrote, and scrawled his signature across the imprint, before repeating the process on the back of my travel permit.

The policeman folded the sheet back into its origami-like creases and slipped it into my passport. I squinted as we walked out into the growing heat, still no closer to ascertaining where Omar lived or, indeed, if he was actually in town. I wandered past the trio of seated men just as one of them, his face puckered with concentration, took a deep suck on the dying stub. As we stepped out of the police compound, my companion indicated that he would make enquiries of two men who were seated on a bench in the square. The elder of the two, a sinewy man with a bony face suggesting Arab blood, was called Ali Elhaggi Ousmane and I learned that he held some form of civic office. Not only did he know Omar, but he told us he was expected back from the desert that afternoon. The sun prickled the nape of my neck and, as the minutes passed, I felt a smear of sweat gently gathering on my brow.

'I know somewhere you can stay,' Ali Elhaggi benignly suggested. 'The Health Minister has a house here,' he continued. 'His uncles sometimes use it. Just tell them that I sent you. If I see Omar I will say you're there.'

I gratefully accepted the proposition and my long-suffering companion and I walked off in search of the minister's lodgings.

We wound our way through meandering alleys, between sepia walls randomly dotted with closed doorways. Reflected heat from the bone-coloured sand triggered an itching around the collar; our steps sank into the ground as if it was a beach and my calf muscles tightened reflexively. We eventually stopped outside a metal gate, and a boy let us into a courtyard where a square bungalow nestled within the confines of a perimeter wall. My companion spoke to an elderly, wizened Tubu and I heard Ali Elhaggi's name being mentioned. I was led through a narrow hall into a spacious reception room where four sofas were pushed up against the walls. The boy hastily swept some rubbish into the corner of a room beyond it, then turned over a mattress from which, as it collapsed back onto the floor, particles of dust, like clouds of spores from decomposing puffballs, detonated into the shredded shafts of light.

I thanked my companion, gave him some crumpled notes and watched him leave in his characteristic hurried, shuffling manner. I felt the elderly Tubu studying me and, after he gestured with a slow sway of his right arm that this was my room I indicated, by putting my hands to my left cheek as if they were a pillow and tilting my head into them, that I would try and sleep. He smiled, nodded gracefully and left. I gently closed the door, simply pleased I had secured a safe space and surveyed my surroundings. They were illuminated by a window with two metal shutters and, apart from a couple of rugs and a large bound copy of the Qur'an propped on a wooden stand with some accompanying prayer beads, the room was bare. I unscrewed the plastic cap of a bottle of water, put the nozzle between my lips, contentedly gulped the warm liquid, kicked off my Timberland shoes and then, lying prostrate on the mattress, exhaled deeply and fell into a blissful sleep.

*   *   *

I awoke with that permeating furry sensation, sometimes found when slumber follows a period of unrelenting exertion or sleep deprivation, as if you and your body are, for a moment, slightly detached from each other. Yet, within that ephemeral detachment, I felt wholly secure in my new environment. Somewhere nearby, the muezzin chanted the azan, and his melodious summons blended with the soothing babble of small children playing outside the window:

> *Allāhu Akbar* [God is most great]
> *Ashhadu anna la ilāha illa Allāh* [I bear witness there is no God but God]
> *Ashhadu anna Muḥammadan rasūl Allāh* [I bear witness Muhammad is the prophet of God]
> *Hayya 'alā al-ṣalāt* [Come to prayer]
> *Hayya 'alā al-falāḥ* [Come to well-being]
> *Allāhu akbar* [God is most great]
> *Lā ilāha illa Allāh* [There is no God but God]

*   *   *

Omar arrived after the evening ṣalāt dressed in a slate-coloured robe and yellow turban. Smiling broadly, he clasped my hands and introduced his interpreter, Mohammed, a young man in his early twenties who wore a cinnamon robe.

'*Bonne arrivée*,' Mohammed grinned. 'We will buy the camels tomorrow,' he continued, in surprisingly fluent French.

As we eased ourselves into the cushioning folds of a sofa, four elderly Tubu arrived, their wrinkled faces gleaming like polished metal. With a hushed rustling of their robes, they settled into the remaining seats, where they sat silent and motionless, radiating a timeless sagacity.

I unfolded the map and, as Omar spoke, he drew his finger across the Manga's grid squares that skimmed beneath the 16th parallel.

'Have any other white people been through this region by camel?' I asked.

'*Jamais*,' Omar swiftly replied, and then gabbled something to Mohammed.

'Omar says,' Mohammed continued, 'that although a few tourists travel by jeep between Agades and Nguigmi, the region you will be travelling through is virgin territory for *un blanc*, as you will be cutting across country.'

'Are you,' I turned to Mohammed, 'coming with us?'

'No,' he replied. 'You will meet your interpreter tomorrow.'

It was dark outside by the time we finished our conversation, and we agreed it would be best – because I was white – if Omar bought the camels at the market without me. I was told Ahmet – the interpreter – would meet me at 2 o'clock the following afternoon, once Omar had secured the camels, and we would then go to the market. I removed the sleeved wads of notes hidden under the protective foam of my metal camera case, and Omar carefully counted the sum that had been agreed in Niamey for the purchase of the camels, saddles and supplies for the trip across the Manga. 'Omar asks,' Mohammed translated, 'if you want to be there when he buys the supplies?'

'No,' I replied. 'I trust him.'

Omar looked slightly surprised, but pleased by my response and, before leaving, he asked Mustapha – the boy who had earlier tidied up my room – to take me to where I could find something to eat.

I zipped up my fleece and followed Mustapha into the murky night. The rutted pavements were freckled with the orange glow of charcoal burners where the shadows of robed forms stood, or hunched over smouldering embers. The Tubu drifted through the blackness as if they belonged to another world, briefly appearing and then disappearing – fragments of motion – and there was a noticeable absence of raised voices or clatter as we strolled past a row of stalls selling tins of food, millet and bread. Mustapha led me into a hut where a skinny man, dressed in a T-shirt and dirty, faded jeans, sliced an onion next to a sizzling pan. Behind him, a figure huddled over a metal dish, scooping up a diminishing pile of black beans with a spoon.

Sitting down I watched the cook crack open a couple of eggs. He whisked them into a froth, which he poured into a scalding pan. The flames erupted and then receded as the yellow liquid congealed. It had been two days since my last meal. I watched the steaming omelette slide from the pan onto a metal dish, and monitored its progress from the stove to the table with hungry anticipation. A robust-looking man in his mid-thirties then stepped into the eatery. He wore a brown robe, his head was swaddled in a white turban, and his skin was a shade somewhere between ebony and amber.

'*Assalam Alaykum,*' he said to me, his eyes glinting in the flickering reflection of stove flames.

'*Alaykum Assalam,*' I replied, or rather wanted to reply. What actually came out was a jumbled mess and I knew it. He smiled at me, I think pleased that I had tried, and then melted back into the darkness with the bag he had come to collect. I am not a polyglot, but I realised I would have to add to my flawed French not only a few Islamic courtesies, but also a Tubu vocabulary. On top of that, there was the small matter of having to master a camel.

10

Ahmet Elhadji Nour arrived at 2 o'clock wearing a snowy robe draped over his wiry frame; a matching turban coiled about his crown, its folds swathed around the jawbone. The colour contrast – between textile and skin pigment – threw the details of his angular features into relief and, when he smiled, any sense of austerity was banished by an overall gentleness; yet behind those dark eyes, there appeared to be a sadness that hinted at some distant episode. There was a sheen on the back of his elegant, nut-brown hands, and the skin beneath his fingernails was a delicate pink.

A sunbeam illuminated the hall as we made our introductions, which were spiced with silent assessment. Ahmet spoke in rapid sentences, and his accent had a nasal twang, as if spoken by someone from Marseille. And then it was time to go to the market. Aware of the burgeoning heat, I wrapped around my head an olive-green turban, and we stepped out of the cool, cavernous bungalow into a hazy white glare that had stolen the sun. The reflected light seemed amplified under a sky the colour of manganese and, as we wandered along the snaking alleys, funnelling gusts showered our progress with sand.

Whereas Agades, inside or out, had been covered with sepia-coloured dust, everything in Nguigmi was tinted white, so that the many children scampering about looked as though their faces, legs, arms and feet were painted with liquid chalk. The town itself did not appear to have been designed, but just to have arisen out of the sand. With loudspeakers notably absent, the muezzin's velvety notes drifted over the settlement, like willow-down floating across a summer evening sky. As the azan hung over Nguigmi, it felt like an invitation to sense the soul beyond the relentless distractions of daily life – the idea of a human need to revisit stillness and regain a feeling of alignment.

The alleys and buildings started to dwindle as we walked on, and the unfolding vista revealed the blurry bustle of the market, activity that was obscured by a haze, as if enveloped in a milky membrane. We walked across an area of dead ground that separated the domestic from the commercial. Ahead lay a cacophony of growls and grunts. In front of three long tiers of stalls, hundreds of tethered and hobbled dromedaries were gathered and, between them, robed individuals conversed or strolled underneath the sauropod-like necks. The dromedaries were of all ages and huddled together in groups, and there were perhaps five hundred of them chaperoned by their Tubu and Arab masters. It was, apparently, an average Sunday market turnout, and there could be as many as one thousand dromedaries for sale on any one day.

The Tubu always referred to the dromedaries as 'camels', and from here on so will I, if for no other reason than that 'camel' is visually and tonally more attractive. 'Dromedary' seems to dribble when pronounced, as if spoken with one's mouth full. Not only that, but the very word seems somehow misapplied, as if it should belong in the sphere of entomology. However, it all makes sense, because the other name for a dromedary is 'Arabian camel', and they would have travelled here along the Old Salt Road. The Manga camels do not live much beyond twenty-five years and are either used for the transport of goods, riding or breeding; they are often sold after the salt and date run to Bilma and, if not destined for Libya, sometimes end up in Kano; so a camel born in the Manga could cross the length and breadth of the Sahara and journey to the Mediterranean, even the Atlantic, before finally having known several owners and ending its days carrying reed mats in northern Nigeria.

Ahmet explained that the majority of camels for sale were from the region of Tasker, on the other side of the Manga, and were destined for Libya. One brawny camel driver, Hessene

Abdoulkarim, explained to Ahmet that he had escorted a caravan of two thousand six hundred camels from Nguigmi to Sebha along the Old Salt Road; a desert journey of some one thousand five hundred kilometres, that passed through the Ténéré's salt mines of Bilma and Segedine and, from thence, into the Fezzan across the Murzuq to Sebha – just four hundred kilometres from the Mediterranean's aquamarine waters. Hessene explained it required eight camel drivers to escort two hundred camels and that Nguigmi was the most important camel market, for what appeared to be at least a thousand square miles: on average between two thousand and two thousand five hundred camels were sold each month – a proof this segment of the Old Salt Road was alive and thriving, as it had been for centuries.

It is an exhilarating sensation to wander amongst such a multitude of camels and listen to the disgruntled sounds issuing from their larynxes, as if they are complaining to one another. They groan, roar, bellow, moan, whimper, sigh and hum; it is true, camels do hum, and I came to learn that those tending towards that trait often had a gentler disposition. All of them looked resigned to their role as animals of burden, as if they had contemplated their predicament at length and, realising there was no escape, settled for subordination; a state manifested in their gaze, as if searching for something on the horizon that could never be found.

While Ahmet and I wove beneath the throng of craning serpentine necks, it was as if the camels were somehow superior; with their size and lofty viewpoint on the world, they appeared to maintain a certain autonomy. As with humans, it was sometimes possible to see which camels had been psychologically scarred by their experiences, but those cases seemed to be rare, as the nomads think about the needs of their animals' stomachs before their own. Some camels simply stood quietly amid the ruckus, looking slowly from left to right, as if the conversation was beneath them and they had heard it all before. The younger ones behaved like new apprentices, tongue-tied and slightly in awe, while the few calves huddled between the legs of their mothers, as if hiding in a cave.

The tail of my turban flapped in a passing dust squall, as Ahmet and I strolled through the melee. Many Tubu came up to greet my guide – each of whom I was introduced to – and, on each occasion, they reciprocated with nodding heads and benevolent smiles; their eyes sparkling with that wilderness sheen. It was simple to identify the Arabs among the confusion of robed figures, as they were noticeably shorter in stature; sometimes only half the size of the Tubu. Their skin was amber, their eyes were narrower and they looked, even at a distance, as if they belonged to a different ethnic category and culture, despite the smiles and common garb; they also carried themselves differently, and appeared segregated in the colourful swirl of activity that was dominated by Tubu.

Beyond the market, and behind the profusion of camels, was a smaller area allocated for the sale of goats, donkeys and horses, the last smaller in size than Mongolian ponies. They were shepherded by a handful of Fulani who were distinguishable from both the Tubu and the Arabs by their taller and leaner build. They seemed, aside from commercial endeavour, to confine their company to their own people. Whereas the Tubu and Arabs were the Manga camel breeders, it appeared that the Fulani, or Peul, were only interested in goats and donkeys. I was unable to discover who was responsible for the breeding of horses, although they appeared to be of only marginal interest, since camels were, by some measure, the preferred method of transport.

Robed figures idly wandered between the huts, scrutinising metal tubs of dried dates, garlic cloves, salt, corn, flour, peanuts, dried tomatoes and red chilli peppers, Sahelian cooking herbs, pips to flavour tea, onion leaves and a dried vegetable product that, apparently, Tubu women used to perfume their hair. Some stalls sold textiles for robes and turbans, while others offered the usual tins of tuna, sardines, pasta and biscuits. Further along was a row of branch-covered huts where daggers were being forged and soldered in the searing heat of charcoal fires.

Alongside those individuals who were hammering blades into shape, young men crouched in the sand crafting scabbards and dagger handles; the leather sheaths were dyed cerise and liquorice. The handles were plaited, like a wicker basket, and banded with three brassy coils; protruding from the butt was a blunt spoon-shaped piece of metal, suggesting that, if the blade was immobilised in the grasp of an opponent, the nub could be lethally withdrawn into the face. A hook of leather was tied into the back of the metal hilt and, into it, a leather strap was designed to be fastened around the left biceps; the elder men, however, wore their daggers around the waist, and I wondered if that was a generational trend.

Neighbouring stalls sold bows and arrows, lances and tasselled camel whips twined with verdigris, maroon, black and mustard stitching. Ahmet recommended that I purchase robes for the journey across the Manga because, as he put it, my clothes were *encombrant* (cumbersome) and, as we discussed this, an adolescent who was sharpening daggers in front of us reached out his right hand towards me. In his fingers was a large silver coin with a hole through the top, as if it had been used as a medallion. As I turned it over in my palm, I saw that one side was decorated with the Hapsburg crest and on the other was the bust of Maria Theresa, Holy Roman Empress, Archduchess of Austria, and Queen of Hungary and Bohemia. It bore the date 1780.

I turned to Ahmet. 'Can you ask him where he got this from?'

'He says his great-grandfather acquired it from an Arab, and it's been a family heirloom ever since.'

'Is he sure he wants to sell this?'

'Yes,' Ahmet replied after translating my question. 'I will find out how much he wants for it along with the dagger we were looking at.'

I bought both the dagger and the coin and, as we strolled off in search of a tailor, Ahmet explained that many coins were melted down to make jewellery. I was to discover later that Maria Theresa thalers were for a long period the most widely accepted coinage in many parts of the world, especially Africa. As a result they were minted for over one hundred and fifty years in many places, from Birmingham to Bombay, and all inscribed with the same year: 1780. Who was to know where and when the coin I had in my hand might have originated? But I still wondered about all that antique coinage which had ended up being smelted in a region with centuries-old links to Barbary and the Mediterranean to finish its journey making many a Tubu bangle.

11

For at least two thousand years, the caravan routes of the Sahara, as invisible as underground rivers, linked the Mediterranean to the Sahel. The Romans sourced their elephants and hippos from Lake Chad, and in 1960 an Edward III coin was found south-west of Kano, further testimony to the ancient transit between the north African littoral and the sub-Saharan kingdoms. For centuries the Algerian, Tangerine, Sallentine, Tripolitan and Tunisian pirates raided the shipping traffic between Europe and the Levant, and – at a very conservative estimate – a million and a half Caucasians ended up as slaves in Barbary. Although the sea rovers never fully recovered after the Battle of Lepanto in October 1571 – when the twenty-four-year-old Don Juan of Austria and his fellow commanders defeated the Ottoman armada – their nimble, three-master xebecs and oar-galleys menaced the seas with a relentless ferocity: the Algerines alone of the corsair regencies, according to slave counts, captured two hundred and forty-eight thousand Europeans between 1640 and 1683, and it was not until the capitulation of Algiers on 5 July 1830 that the Mediterranean was finally rid of the Barbary marauders.

Slavery, like disease, did not discriminate between creed or colour, as Moors, whites and blacks alike were, depending on their situation, sold in the slave markets of Barbary, Europe, the Caribbean or America. Livorno, in north-west Italy on the Ligurian Sea, was, as *The Barbary Slaves* author Stephen Clissold puts it, 'a slave market scarcely less important than that of Algiers', and the tally of slaves plundered from the West

African coast for the New World's sugar plantations and cotton fields rocketed from nine hundred thousand in the sixteenth century to four million in the nineteenth century. Throughout that period slaves, like camels, trudged subserviently along the network of worn tracks that span the Sahara.

European countries often brokered brittle treaties with the Barbary corsairs. The one signed on 5 April 1686 between Britain and Algiers stipulated: 'That henceforward no subject of His Majestie of Great Britain shall be bought or sold or made slaves in any part of the Kingdom of Algiers, upon any pretence whatsoever.' It seems plausible that the first Caucasians to penetrate the Sahel did so as slaves.

Paul Imbert, who travelled with his master from Morocco to the Sudan in 1612, did so long before nineteenth-century explorers began their expeditions. One extraordinary account I stumbled across related to a Franciscan brother, Pieter Farde, who was allegedly captured by Algerians on his way to Jerusalem in October 1686. He was taken to Bona (Annaba), sold into slavery and travelled to Agades; he was freed, robbed and stripped in the Sahel and picked up by a caravan. He then became the sole survivor of a shipwreck, lived on a reef-like outcrop in the South Atlantic, was rescued by pirates and eventually returned to his convent in Ghent, where, only five months later, he died, aged thirty-nine. His letters recounting this odyssey were published in 1706, fifteen years after his death. I originally dismissed them as a fraud, until discovering that the events he described corresponded with geographical and historical fact.

Missives written in 1686 from the English consul in Algiers to the Earl of Sunderland confirmed that ships were captured as suggested in Farde's letters; that letters written by white slaves in Barbary did in fact make their way to Europe, as surviving accounts in archives reveal; that Farde's description, after his emancipation, of a then-unexplored Sahelian sector of the Old Salt Road was accurate; that the island he describes where he lived like a Robinson Crusoe, although not marked on any map of the time, was probably one of the rocky islets in the broad vicinity of St Helena; and that it is possible to survive on raw fish and rainwater.

These investigations led me to the eleventh-century Franciscan convent in Ghent, rebuilt in 1653, from which Farde set off for his ill-fated journey to Palestine. The building was designed to house a hive of Franciscans but, when it was sold in 2004, only six elderly brothers were left in residence. At the time of my visit, the vaulted cloisters, refectory and cells had changed little since the seventeenth century, but the decline was absolute: the walls were peeling, fractured floorboards were randomly exposed like the bones of a mummified corpse and the corridors were cluttered with detritus. The convent, which Pieter Farde would have once known so well, was in a deplorable state: abandoned, decaying and gloomy.

The following day, I drove to the Franciscan house in St Truiden, where the surviving records from the convent in Ghent had been subsequently stored. An elderly curator opened the arched wooden door beside an adjoining church, and I followed him along a corridor into the cloisters. The edifice appeared to be a replica of the convent in Ghent and was seemingly empty of people and devoid of sound. I was led up some stairs and asked to wait outside a doorway. A few minutes later, an ageing Franciscan, Josef Baetens, arrived and invited me into a rectangular room where antiquarian books and manuscripts were stacked in shelves around the walls.

Baetens explained there were only twenty-two Franciscans living in the convent; he was the youngest at seventy-two. He had heard about Pieter Farde and led me up the few steps into the cramped archives, where row upon row of books were stored as if in a public library. While I leafed through the pages of a pamphlet, Baetens shuffled to the other end of the room and unearthed two shoeboxes containing papers relating to Farde. I sat down at a desk beneath a large window, removed the box lids and carefully began to examine the sheets. A short while later, my left hand reached for a document wrapped in brown paper.

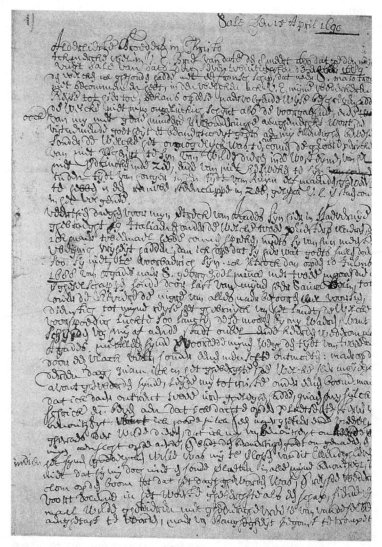

Figure 1 Farde's letter of 15 April 1690 from the corsair port of Sale

At what seemed to be the same instant, and without looking at my hand or the document, I glanced over at Josef Baetens.

'This is it,' I murmured instinctively. 'This is one of his letters.'

I removed the protective paper, and inside it found Pieter Farde's original sixth letter, sent from the corsair port of Salé on 15 April 1690. The letter, written in umber ink, ran to a dozen pages and the leaves were stained a muddy yellow from age. The words, like his sentences, were small and tightly packed as if each letter had been meticulously penned to maximise the space available, and I could see from the grimy, yet distinct crease lines on the blank back page that the letter had, at some time, been folded into four – presumably by Farde – to make the package as small as possible for any person taking the responsibility of forwarding it. The last, fragile page bore his signature. Returning to the opening paragraphs I made out the name Agades written in elegant Flemish script.

Almost a century and a half after that letter was written, on 23 February 1822, a British mission left Tripoli on a three-year quest to discover the source of the Niger. The expedition, consisting of Major Dixon Denham, Hugh Clapperton and Dr Walter Oudney, also set out to fill in some of the spaces beneath the Sahara that were still blank on the African map. The African Association, founded on 9 June 1788, believed the exploration of Niger 'might possibly open to Britain a commercial passage to rich and populous nations.' As the author E.W. Bovill explains:

> Consuls and merchants on the Barbary shore knew no more about the origins of gold, ivory, ebony, pepper and 'Moroccan' leather, which toiling caravans poured into their ports from the remote interior, than did Guinea traders about the sources of slaves, gold, ivory and gum on which they grew rich.

A year later, after a detour to the Murzuq, the mission passed through Nguigmi, on 6 February 1823, on their way to Kuka. They were to spend the following year exploring the region. Denham wrote on 21 May 1823:

Ever since my return from Mandara, an expedition, to be commanded by the Sheikh in person, had been in agitation against a numerous people to the west called Munga (Manga)... It was reported, and with truth, that they could bring twelve thousand bowmen into the field; by far the most efficient force to be found in the black country.

But the explorers never made it into the Manga. When Manga tribesman attacked Kabshary, a settlement apparently situated some hundred and fifty kilometres west of Diffa, the mission retreated east. Towards the end of that year, while Clapperton and Oudney went west to search for the source of the Niger, Denham joined a slave-raiding expedition and was captured. Like Pieter Farde, he too was stripped but managed to escape while his captors bickered over his clothes. Oudney, aged thirty-two, died on 12 January 1824 but, as was later recounted, Clapperton continued west and reached Kano later that month:

Arrayed in naval uniform, I made myself as smart as circumstances would permit... At 11 o'clock we entered Kano, the great emporium of the kingdom of Hausa; but I had no sooner passed the gates, than I felt grievously disappointed; for from the flourishing description of it given by the Arabs, I expected to see a city of surprising grandeur: I found, on the contrary, the houses nearly a quarter of a mile from the walls, and in many parts scattered into detached groups, between large stagnant pools of water. I might have spared all the pains I had taken with my toilet; for not an individual turned his head round to gaze at me, but all, intent on their own business, allowed me to pass by without notice or remark.

The surviving members of the mission, Denham noted in his journal, again travelled through Nguigmi on 27 August 1824 on their return journey to Tripoli:

We were overtaken by so dreadful a storm that we halted and pitched the tent on a high sand-hill within five miles of N'Gygami

[Nguigmi]. Near this hill we had a beautiful view of the open lake, with several islands when the storm cleared away... For safety we all slept outside the huts of N'Gygami: this ground is the highest part of the borders of the lake, and here deep water commences immediately off the shore, while, in some parts, miles of marsh are to be waded through previous to arriving at the lake.

Henry Barth, who bypassed the Manga, travelled thirty-one years later through Nguigmi on the last leg of his five-year odyssey across the Sahara. On 22 May 1855 he recounted:

Thus we reached the new village of Ngegimi, which was built on the slope of the hills, the former town having been entirely swept away by the inundation. Here we remained the forenoon of the following day; the encampment being enlivened by a great number of women from the village, offering for sale fish in a fresh and dried state, besides a few fowls, milk and *temmari*, the seeds of the cotton plant. But with the exception of a few beads for adorning their sable persons, they were scarcely willing to receive anything besides corn. After a short conversation with the chief of the place, the May-Ngegimibe, we set out in the afternoon and, proceeding at a slow rate, as the camels were very heavily laden we passed, after a march of about eight miles, along a large open creek of the *lagune*; and having met some solitary travellers coming from Kanem, encamped about eight in the evening, on rather uneven ground, and kept alternate watch during the night.

The discoveries made by those official pioneers of Sahelian exploration replaced enigma with fact and, in doing so, along with the findings of Mungo Park, Dr Livingstone, Sir Henry Morton Stanley and others, laid down the stepping stones for what was later dubbed: 'The Scramble for Africa'.

The blueprint of that scramble was conceived at the Berlin Conference on 26 February 1885. The international agreement, in which each European country except Switzerland was represented, made it clear that rivalries over African soil were not thought serious enough to justify a European war. The

Treaty was an extraordinary document, where Europe's pleni-potentiaries dissected the African continent without any regard to its indigenous peoples.

Seventeen years after the Berlin Conference, ninety per cent of Africa was under European control. General Gustave Borgnis-Desbordes, the governor-general of Senegal, observed in 1891:

> In Africa, as in Europe, the only irresistible argument is force. Today the blacks are well aware that a peaceful expedition by a white man is only the prelude to a merciless and unceasing commercial exploitation. They take up arms in self-defence and who can blame them?

On occasion the French too did not behave well. In November 1898 Captain Paul Voulet and Lieutenant Charles Chanoine set out west from Koulilkoro, four hundred miles up the Niger from Timbuktu, and embarked on a murderous spree of atrocities across the Sahel as far as west of Zinder. Their rampage lasted until July of the following year, when they were eventually killed. 'Now I am an outlaw,' Voulet raved, a few days before he was shot. 'I renounce my family, my country. I am no longer a Frenchman – I am a black chief.'

With the signing of a 'treaty of peace' between France and the Ahagaar Tuareg on 25 August 1905, the conquest of the Sahara was complete and its landscape and peoples were assimilated into French administration. France established several military outposts in southern Niger in the late 1890s, but did not occupy Agades until 1904, mostly due to the dissident Tuaregs. In 1900 Niger was made a military colony within the Upper Senegal–Niger and in 1922 it became an entity within French West Africa. Under colonialism the Tuaregs were driven into forced labour, conscripted and dispossessed of their lands, which led to a war against the French in 1917 and, conse-quently, to the forced evacuation of the Tuaregs from the Aïr Mountains. As Francis Rennell Rodd, the anthropologist who lived with the Aïr Tuareg in 1922, observed:

Depopulation in the Aïr allowed the desert to encroach. Wells fell in, gardens went out of tillage, and the livestock of the country, more especially the camel herds, were reduced to a fraction of what they had been... In 1922 the policy of the French was reversed, but one is inclined to wonder whether it was not already too late.

In 1926 the colonial capital was transferred from Zinder to Niamey, and Niger remained a French colony until the country achieved independence in 1960. Since that period, the Manga had become a forgotten territory and, from the few accounts I had heard, the way of life there remained as it had been long before any nineteenth-century Europeans penetrated the Sahel.

12

'Why is it called the Manga?'

'Because,' Ahmet replied, as we strolled along an alleyway of stalls in search of some robes, 'the people who lived there were called "Manga".'

'Do they still live there?'

'No,' he answered. 'They have gone.'

'What happened to them?'

'I don't know. I don't think anyone knows.'

We stopped outside a small hut, where we found an Arab cutting a ribbon with a large pair of scissors; beside him, another man stitched a cobalt cuff. I stooped through the entrance into a space lined with rolls of dyed textiles. There was nothing too ornate or garish, just a simple spectrum of colours, yet, having never before thought about a desert fashion, I felt surprisingly self-conscious about my impending choice. I looked around to see what the Tubu wore as they wandered past but, in doing this, I became even more confused. I might have settled for white but, as Ahmet was dressed in that already, it didn't seem appropriate and the dark browns, yellows, greens and blues appeared too loud. I selected a pale lavender material – a choice both Ahmet and the Arab seemed to approve – and while my measurements were being taken, we were told that my outfit would be ready for collection in the morning.

As we returned to the throng of hobbled camels, I learned that Ahmet had seven brothers, seven sisters, three half-brothers and three half-sisters. The oldest sibling was fifty and the youngest, a half-sister, was ten years old, and most of them lived in the desert. A sudden outburst of roaring interrupted us, as a dust pillar whirled through the herd. The Tubu continued, intermittently, to greet Ahmet, and after a while we spotted Omar's distinctive yellow turban, and filed through the camels to find him fastening a canvas sack onto a wooden saddle. He smiled when he saw us and, completing the knot he was tying, glanced up at me and then spoke to Ahmet.

'These are two of your camels,' Ahmet translated. 'The third is over there,' he continued, pointing to the other side of the market, which was slowly disappearing in an expanding veil of dust.

The two male camels, aged five and six, sat quietly in the sand; jaws grinding on piano-key-like teeth and ears revolving like old battleship radar-dishes, as if tuning in to some fragment of overheard camel gossip. The paler of the two gave out a random hum, as if in contemplation. We walked across the market to the third camel, which, as Omar endeavoured to untie a saddle, twisted its neck backwards, hissed and bellowed. Then, like a cobra, it lunged at the human meddling with its flank, yet stopped just short of the turban, as if trying to establish the parameters of a relationship with its new master. Omar, unperturbed by the action, exclaimed in annoyance and swatted the vast head, as if it were a fly. This twelve-year-old camel, another male, was larger and bore a number of healed scars on its back, where the hair had been unable to regenerate.

'Omar suggests,' Ahmet said, 'that you ride this camel because you are bigger.'

'Thanks,' I replied, looking at what I perceived to be a highly belligerent means of transport. 'I might ride one of the others – if that's all right?'

Ahmet translated, and Omar nodded. 'He says that's fine, and that he will ride the big white camel.'

Ahmet explained that we would be leaving with a caravan the following afternoon and that, until then, a camel driver would attend to our three camels. We left Omar and began the walk back to the minister's house. As I strolled beside my guide, I discovered there were three types of Arab who lived in the Manga: the Chouwa Arabs, who arrived from Libya in

1940; the Hasnaui Arabs, who, it seemed, had always been in Niger; and the Mahimide Arabs, who had been arriving from Chad since 1980. I also learned that, in 1996, Ahmet was elected into political office under Niger's Fourth Republic. He served as a politician for two and a half years and, since 2005, had been one of Nguigmi's community councillors.

*   *   *

The next day, the afternoon azan soared across the desert settlement and, in the courtyard, Mustapha's Islamic murmurings hovered like early evening bird-song. I pulled on my new, baggy, pyjama-like trousers and donned a knee-length blue cotton shirt. Over these, I slipped on the long pale lavender robe that fell from the shoulders to my ankles, and carefully wrapped a white turban into place in a manner that, on this occasion, left my face exposed. As I stepped out of the room, Mustapha grinned and nodded in quiet approval. I wandered outside to find Omar and Ahmet with our supplies and the three camels. They declined my offer to help, and I returned to collect my backpack and knapsack, which contained my all-important water bottle: an ultra-filtration unit that removed bacteria, viruses, cysts, parasites, fungi and all other waterborne pathogens.

One of the white canvas sacks being strapped onto the camels contained our food: pasta, tuna, sardines, Chinese tea and sugar. Another was stuffed with dried dates. There were a couple of jerrycans filled with water, and two further tubes of water that were tied at both ends like goatskins. And then there was my backpack, which, after being wrapped up in a leather sheet, neatly occupied one side of a camel's flank. Our supplies and belongings were fastened onto the wooden camel frames, so that each side was carefully balanced, and a conifer-green canvas tarpaulin was thrown over it all. We then positioned our blankets in the middle as cushions.

The camels lurched to their feet and we led them along a potholed road that became a sandy lane bordered by courtyard walls. As we walked up the slight incline, the chalky ground and sepia buildings were framed by an azure sky until, over the summit, the path curled to the right and Nguigmi started to melt into the surrounding wilderness. Maybe it was the sound of the camels' muffled steps, the clicking of their ankle tendons, the slow, hydraulic-like movement of their heels sinking into the sand as the large rotund hooves splayed out, but, quite quickly, I began to observe the scene from another perspective. It was as if we were leaving a rural harbour on an extended ocean journey, and everything that had been familiar a few hours previously now belonged to a different realm.

We soon arrived at an overgrown oasis on the town's northernmost fringe: a copse of date palms, acacias and lush vegetation where, beneath drooping branches, children played in a muddy pond and the air was filled with a ragged chorus of happy chatter. Collected beside the turbid water was a group of nine robed and veiled Tubu men in their early twenties with their camels; they wore daggers fixed around the left bicep or across the chest and, as we approached them, Ahmet explained that they were returning to their home villages. We would be travelling with them for the initial leg of our trip across the Manga.

Ahmet tugged the rein downwards and his camel groaned as it sank to the ground, its legs neatly folding up beneath it. Following suit, as I had been shown, I instructed mine to do the same. Our companions' belongings were organised, like ours, in meticulous arrangement on their camels. Their robes were an assortment of golden-yellow, chestnut, reed-green, black and aquamarine, and their turbans were equally varied in colour; some of the riders had cross-hilted swords neatly tucked along their camel's flank. The air smelt of dirty, tepid water and warm foliage and, as children splashed and crashed through the miry water, our quiet conversations were framed among a tumult of squeals, yelps and giggles.

Late afternoon shadows, like a shawl of frayed muslin, crept towards us. The sun's glow faded, and a silent shift could be felt. It was time to leave. The Tubu were on the move and our tranquil surroundings erupted with the roars of disgruntled camels, as they lay down to be mounted by their riders.

13

The camels lurched to their feet and, one by one, our companions began to drift towards the wilderness. I felt, for the first time, that extraordinary sensation of being thrust backwards and then forwards as the animal struggled to get up. Then, with my legs unskilfully straddling the camel's shoulder blades, I rode beside Ahmet to take our places in the cavalcade.

We followed a sandy track that spun away from Nguigmi. I saw the last outbuildings disappear behind us, and, quite quickly, we were engulfed by the seemingly endless landscape. I hooked the inside of my right leg around the pommel, so that my right calf and foot fell alongside my left thigh. We swayed in motion with our camels, while the surroundings floated past, as if we were travelling at sea.

In quiet conversation, I learned that Ahmet was born in the bush in 1966. He had no idea of the exact date or even the month: the Tubu, I discovered, did not recognise birthdays. He had been married twice and had a couple of daughters and two sons.

'When the Tubu get divorced,' he quipped with a twinkle, 'they have a party to celebrate.'

As the shimmering sun sedately descended towards the horizon and a shadowy net was cast over the Sahel, a cluster of crispy, honey-coloured leaves skittered across the sand towards us and I pulled the turban across my mouth. We had only been in the saddle for an hour when we arrived at the lip of a shallow escarpment ringed by a loose growth of spindly acacias and spiky bushes. Our companions settled about thirty metres away and we made our camp beside a protective wall of shrubbery. The camels were unloaded, hobbled and left to graze among the straggly vegetation, while shallow holes were scooped into the sand and kindling fires lit. The placid tints of dusk were momentarily shattered as, bickering over a sprig, the big white camel bit another camel's face and left an ugly, bloody gash where the skin had been peeled back across the length of the jawbone. The two animals were quickly separated and steered towards different trees. Stillness returned and the first stars began to appear.

'*Tu bois, quand je bois,*' Omar stipulated in one of his rare forays into French, and I nodded in assent. I was happy to obey. I would drink when he did. I knew my body was going to change and there was no better way to adapt than to copy their survival techniques. As I laid out a camel blanket, I could see the sand was covered with what Ahmet and Omar called *cram-crams*: creamy barbellate pods, the size of a garden pea, which looked like spores viewed under the microscope. In the softest breeze they flurried over the sandy surface like dispersing pollen, and their barbels detached from the pods so that walking barefoot was impossible – like shards of glass, they invisibly penetrated skin and clothes.

'Omar must return to Nguigmi,' Ahmet announced. 'He has forgotten the radio and we need to keep in touch with the world – because of the rebellion.'

I watched Omar mount his camel and vanish into the blackness.

'Will he be able to find his way back?' I enquired.

'He'll return soon,' Ahmet replied, prodding the charcoal with a stick into a bowl of ruby embers. Another group of Tubu emerged from the shadows and dismounted beside a bush between the two islands of campfires. As they unloaded their possessions, nomadic faces glistened in the firelight, and the strumming of a lyre's velvety notes arose from the fireside of our neighbours.

A while later, Ahmet poured some water into a sooty pot that resembled a miniature cauldron, which he secured on the charcoal bed; he then scraped a separate trench beside the fire and, after transferring a mound of embers between the ends of two sticks, he wedged a red teapot above the heat. I sat opposite, slicing an onion. As he cut the meat away from a skinned goat's leg with his dagger, vapours swirled like rising mountain mist above the simmering pot, and I nibbled a chewy dried date that tasted as if it had been caramelised.

Omar re-appeared out of the desert night, silent and ghostly. Ahmet flicked on the radio, twisted the antennae into position, and we ate to a French broadcaster's bulletins.

* * *

The following day began before dawn, when Omar murmured a hushed ṣalāt; and then, after a pause, came the cosy sound of a crackling fire. In the freezing desert air, I tugged my blanket tighter around me. Omar and Ahmet huddled around flames warming their hands as if washing them, and a funnel of steam chugged from the teapot's nozzle. I filled my metal mug with water, placed it on a crown of embers and waited for it to boil; Omar stirred a pot, and Ahmet filtered Chinese tea from it until he was content with its colour and viscosity; two glass thimbles were then filled with the yellow-tinted liquid and shared between the three of us, whereupon the pot was refilled with a new batch of tea and sugar, and the cycle was started all over again. It would take me a few days to realise there was no better rehydration formula than this simple sugary concoction the Tubu regularly drank. For the first few days of our journey we barely needed any water at all.

The stars faded, until there were only a couple left. Then they, too, disappeared, and the morning's pale hues were matched by the mellifluous notes of a finch's solo. While I ate a bowl of Omar's sweetened rice pudding, the melting shroud of mist that draped across the escarpment beneath us revealed a grazing camel and her young calf.

'We have hard riding days ahead of us,' Ahmet said, breaking the silence. 'No stops until dusk, except to water the camels, and a short break for lunch.' I nodded. 'Also,' he continued, 'we have to wait for a couple of hours as one of our companions returned to the market early this morning because they forgot something.'

The sky became cloaked with dust and the sun disappeared into a sodium-like whiteness. Bushes shivered, and formerly listless leaves twisted and flipped like landed mackerel. I tugged the turban over my mouth and the bridge of my nose, and followed Ahmet in search of our camels. We found them, some time later; their necks craning towards twigs, as pouting lips wobbled towards lofty shoots.

We led them back to camp where they were slowly loaded up and, as I was securing my pack, one of the Tubu from the adjoining camp sauntered over. Glancing towards me, he pointed at my dagger lying in the sand and picked it up. He gestured at his own weapon, strapped around his upper arm, and indicated that I should extend my left arm, whereupon he promptly secured the blade into place. Seemingly pleased that I was now properly dressed, he looked me over – and smiled. The group we had arrived with the previous evening rode out of sight in closely knit formation. Ahmet explained that we would meet them at a well in the evening.

It wasn't until midday that our companion returned from Nguigmi and then, finally, we mounted and set off. There were seven of us, with a camel and its six-week-old calf in tow. We rode through the murky landscape, heading towards the sixteenth parallel and, as we did so, the white sun inched over us. By degrees, the terrain lost its Sahelian vegetation, and transformed into an almost lifeless world. In the evolving journey's silent steps, the periscope-like rotation of the camels' necks when they scanned the horizon, and the twitching of their ears, I became aware of a quiet camaraderie that had permeated us all – men and camels; a silent solidarity conceived in the saddle. Like a moving island, the group swayed as one through a hostile land.

14

Ahmet's eyelashes and eyebrows were coated in a film of chalky dust, as if they had been exposed to an Arctic chill, and his ebony-like skin was powdered an ash grey; a composition that softened, but set off, his sinewy visage. As we rode through an increasingly denuded landscape, the afternoon sky was unable to shed its white, dusty mantle and the sun's disc resembled a giant ping-pong ball. There was no bird-song, only a penetrating stillness, like walking through a winter's dawn. For much of the time the caravan travelled silently but, as with a flock of twilight starlings, a minuscule inconsistency would sometimes momentarily hook us together, as if we were one organism. It might have been an infinitesimal shift of rhythm in a camel's step or perhaps a thought that had trembled the psychic airwaves, but whatever the conception of those moments, the immediate vicinity kaleidoscoped and, for an instant, our group was umbilically connected and the senses were, for a fraction of a second, stretched to an extreme clarity. Then the noisy pounding of heartbeats and clamour of breathing would fall away, and we all drifted off again onto our own planes.

We stopped just once that first day – and that was for prayers. While the Tubu hunkered between some sheltered dunes and I wandered out of sight, because I did not want to intrude, I heard the murmurings of 'Allāhu Akbar'. I sat in the sand to ease my back, and began to study the remains of a camel skeleton. The bones seemed to stare back at me, as granules of sand rolled against a rib and began to leapfrog into a miniature dune, and a timid gust twiddled the ailing leaves of a dying bush beside me.

I had thought about naming our camels after some Romans: Augustus, Maecenas and Horace. Like Augustus, the white camel was a bully and the other two were obviously friends – hence the inseparable Maecenas and Horace: politician and writer. However, the Tubu did not name their camels and I had to sell the animals in three weeks' time. So, returning to my companions, I left this thought behind as we all mounted and the camels roared into life. As we rode north, and the sun began its crawling descent towards the west, one of our companions turned on a radio that was strapped to his camel's left flank under a lime-green cloth, and Arabic music blurted out. The dissonant chords provided a certain reference point while we rode, as if the silence needed to be interrupted, to remind us that our group was not absolutely insignificant, and that we did actually exist.

I strained the rope and pulled back into a walk beside Ahmet who was riding alone on the left flank.

'I've read that all this,' I said, 'right up to Lake Chad, was a part of the seventeenth-century sultanate of Agades. I know there was an ancient track the sultan's armies took between Agades and the Termit Mountains, but do you know which path the armies took from there to Lake Chad?'

'I have heard about this, but I don't know the route,' Ahmet replied.

'It was an impressive sultanate, I understand, with Agades in the centre, it stretched to the northern Aïr, as far as Ader in the west, Bornu to the east along the western shores of Lake Chad, and Katsina in the south.'

'We learnt about this at school,' Ahmet answered, his eyes disclosing a glimmer of surprise.

'What was the sultan's name again?' I had forgotten. 'Ah,' I remembered. 'I think it was Muhammad al-Mubarak.'

Although Agades was allegedly founded in 1460, the earliest map I had discovered that mentioned its name was in Ortelius' 1570 *Africae Tabula Nova*. Nearly a century later, Agades is marked five times on Joan Blaeu's *Africae Nova Descriptio*

– as if marking out the peripheries of an empire. It was not uncommon in Arabic for a capital and a country to be called by the same name, and this appeared to be the case when Blaeu's cartographers compiled the information, presumably obtained from sub-Saharan caravans by European consuls stationed in the corsairs' Barbary ports. The inclusions for Agades appear in the shape of an arc across the Sahel, and it is easy to imagine a leathery black finger skirting across the sultanate's boundaries of an incomplete map. What is also revealing is that the entries for Agades are a rough geographical blueprint for those described by Abu Bakar al-Tahir Tashi, a diarist, who was born in Agades in 1657, the same year, as he put it, that 'fire broke out in the house of the Sultan'.

Abu Bakar's diaries cast a rare gleam onto an otherwise impenetrably foggy chapter of the Sahel's history. As an Emagadezi, or a person of Agades, he grew up in the town, became a young scholar there and was familiar with the sultan and his sons. He describes how Agades was an independent city-state, whose sultan, Muhammad al-Mubarak, had ruled the Emagadezi and the Tuaregs since 1654. During the thirty-four years of the sultan's leadership and the military campaigns directed by his son, Muhammad Agg-Abba, the sultanate experienced a period of tribal unity and territorial growth. With control of the Sahara's south-eastern caravan routes, its authority was absolute, and disorder and rebellion were met with swift punitive expeditions. Even though the sultan and his son briefly evacuated Agades because of Tuareg tribal disputes in 1667, they expanded the sultanate's frontiers throughout al-Mubarak's reign. For example, in 1685, their armies 'smashed the people of Zanfara,' Abu Bakar noted. 'They fled in defeat and their best men died. More than a thousand men of the Zanfara died there. God gave victory to the Tuaregs over their enemies.' In a second campaign later that year the sultan's armies 'killed all the chief men of Zanfara and returned to Agades in triumph... After their return plague broke out and there was a great death in Agades.'

Under Muhammad al-Mubarak, Agades thrived and had not seen such a period of prosperity since the early sixteenth century, when it flourished as a tributary state under the Songhay Empire: a power that controlled a region bigger than Europe and was administered from Gao, on the banks of the Niger, in what is today Mali. The Songhay were the Tuaregs' hereditary enemies and had, up until 1493, been ruled for eight centuries by the Za dynasty of Lemta kings, but that was before one of their principal lieutenants defeated the last King of Lemta at the battle of Angoo, near Gao, and Askia the Great promptly proclaimed himself king.

Askia, founder of the Sonike dynasty, was not only a brilliant tactician, but also a political and administrative genius who had an inherent respect for religion and learning. He divided his kingdom into four provinces, each with its own governor, and formed a standing army ready for immediate service. For the next twenty-two years Askia expanded his kingdom and, in 1515, his army captured Agades. He lived there for a year, evicted the majority of the Tuareg residents, replaced them with a Songhay colony and imposed a yearly tribute of 150,000 ducats – all policies that ensured Agades became a stable tributary state. After these achievements, he went back home again.

Agades then became the capital of Sudan's gold trade and, at its zenith, even had its own standard weight for gold. In 1528, blind and worn out, the great Askia was forced to abdicate by a tyrannical son, Musa, who confined him to a palace. Three years later, after Musa's death, his fortunes declined even further, when he was banished, as E.W. Bovill described it, 'to an island on the Niger infested with mosquitoes and frogs'. Askia, the man who had taught his subjects organised government and created one of the greatest empires in pre-colonial Africa, finally died a year later in Gao, after being rescued by another son, Ismail, who went on to rule the Songhay Kingdom.

In 1591, Gao fell to the Moroccan Empire and Agades began to empty, as the gold market crumbled and merchants, along with their families, emigrated south to Kano and Katsina. Since then, only two sultans had ruled Agades before Muhammad al-Mubarak came to power in 1654, after succeeding his father. The Sultan of Bornu besieged and captured Agades, but al-Mubarak retreated to the Aïr's mountain fortress of Bagzane. Here the Tuaregs rallied to him. Over the ensuing three years he resisted the invaders in an aggressive campaign of guerrilla warfare, and the malnourished Bornu soldiers eventually retreated back across the Ténéré desert where, at the oasis of Fashi on the way to Bilma, the Bornu army, abandoned by their sultan, was surprised and defeated by the Tuaregs. It was with the capture of Fashi that the Tuaregs were able to influence, control and develop the salt trade with the Sudan – a lucrative financial artery that replaced Agades' gold vacuum.

On 20 April 1687, a month after the Franciscan Pieter Farde was freed from Agades, Muhammad al-Mubarak died 'between sunset and the Isha prayer,' Abu Bakar recorded in his journal:

> He had held office for thirty-four years. His son assumed authority. He was the eldest, Muhammad Agg-Abba. He did so during that night before daybreak. There was no dispute, nor argument. The people were in full agreement.

The new Sultan had begun his thirty-five-year reign, but with it were sown the seeds of decline, and Agades would never again reach such heights of power. However, by this time, Agades had sprawled to an expansive three and a half miles in circumference, and may have been home to as many as fifty thousand inhabitants. Today, a glance at a map of the old quarter of Agades will reveal not the microchip uniformity of Western urban symmetry, but an image much as it would have looked in 1687: free of harsh lines and replete with non-conforming shapes that, as a composite, resembles a colony of bacteria under the microscope.

*   *   *

Riding across the Manga, discussing the seventeenth-century sultanate of Agades with Ahmet was bewitching and, as the afternoon wore on, our dialogue sifted into lengthy pauses, and slowly fell into a companionable silence. In the dimming light, a small caravan of four camels materialised in front of us, led by an Arab patriarch on a chestnut pony. They had travelled from the Termit Mountains and were on their way to Nguigmi's market with a load of dates, presumably sourced from Bilma. We stopped as Omar and the Arab exchanged greetings and arms were pointed ahead and behind in helpful directions. Then we pulled away again towards an endless panorama of Sahelian undulations, dotted with isolated, messy scrub and the skeletons of skinny acacias.

15

Shortly before dusk we arrived at a well encircled by camel and goat dung. Beyond it were a handful of ragged bushes. Our two groups divided, each steering towards one of the few ailing islands of scrub-like bush, as if they were portside moorings. Camels were unloaded, fires lit and canvas blankets unfurled beneath the protective palisade of rickety scrub. While Omar tended to the fire, Ahmet and I led our three camels to the well, where the other Tubu had gathered. A wooden pulley hung over the cavernous pit that spiralled down through the cinnamon-coloured dirt into the blackness. A rope was draped over a wooden pulley and, attached at its end, was a floppy black membrane in the shape of a rotund bucket. The previous traveller had neatly laid out both rope and bucket beside the well, as if it was etiquette to arrange them for the next caravan. Perhaps, within that philosophy, it was not merely the practicality of ensuring the bucket was never soiled or that the rope did not fall into the well that had been considered, but that the subsequent visitor would interpret, in that tidily prepared rope and bucket, a sense of cultural solidarity and peace of mind in an otherwise inhospitable environment.

The rope was tied onto a camel's wooden saddle and the bucket was dropped into the well with a muted splash. The camel was led forward, taking up the slack, and the filled bucket began its ascent from the inky depths. As it reached the surface, two men carried it to a trough and, to avoid aggressive bickering, animals were guided in turn to the turbid water.

The Tubu who had broken camp ahead of us that morning, emerged out of the dusky grey light with three camels in tow. Like us, they circled a clump of scanty vegetation and settled beside it, before beginning the task of unloading and watering their camels. Ahmet and I returned to where Omar was boiling a pot of water, and I arranged my saddle, pack and knapsack in a semicircle around the top of my blanket.

'What about snakes and scorpions?' I enquired.

'Don't worry,' Ahmet replied. 'They won't bother you.'

I unfurled my turban and reclined into a position that relieved my aching back, while wispy plumes of smoke curled into untidy pleats and, in the fading light, Omar and Ahmet turned towards Mecca in prayer. We were travelling companions in the wilderness. The sense I had had, just a few hours earlier, of perhaps being an intruder at these times was dissolving.

'*Allāhu akbar,*' they murmured with bowed heads, hands at the side; their feet evenly spaced. '*Subhānaka Allāhumma wa-bi-hamdika wa-tabāraka ismuka wa-ta'āla jadduka wa-lā ilāha ghayruka*' [Glory and praise be to You, O God, Your name is blessed and Your power is exalted and there is no God but You].

And their soothing invocations hummed in the dark, like glinting fireflies.

Like yachts moored in a remote island bay, each of the three encampments was a respectful, yet reassuring distance from the others. That night there were fifteen Tubu, twenty camels, a calf and myself; the fires flickered in the blackness and there was a muffled babble of chatter – sometimes punctuated by a twig exploding in the fire. The petulant gusts had fallen away at dusk and stillness had settled over the Sahel. Lacy galaxies were spun across the sky, like silky smoke from a dying fire, and the silhouetted landscape was caressed in a silver sheen.

*   *   *

It was cold the following morning when I heard Omar stirring. Curling the rim of my blanket across my chin, I noticed that

Ahmet was still buried beneath his rug. '*Bismi'llāh al-raḥmān al-raḥīm.*' [In the name of God the Compassionate, the Merciful], Omar murmured. I lay motionless and gazed at the stars' rambling configurations. '*Al-ḥamdu li'llāhi rabb al-'ālamīn.*' [Praise be to God, Lord of the worlds]. '*Iyyāka na'budu wa-iyyāka nasta'īn.*' [It is You we worship and You we seek help from].

After Omar had finished praying, he coughed huskily. The early morning silence was disturbed by the scrape of a match, a whoosh and, moments later, flames that signalled the beginning of another day. Ahmet cleared his throat and whispered prayers. The stars melted into a lilac wash, the teapot hissed and Ahmet poured some sweet tea into a glass.

'I learnt this morning,' he said, 'that we will be travelling with the same guys as yesterday. The others are heading east to a wedding.'

While the sky turned a pale eggshell-blue and the men in each encampment began to load up their camels, Omar buried our campfire's charcoal embers under a pile of sand, as a breeze toyed with a cluster of leaves beside me. And then the dunes' curving lines began to blur, as if smudged with a rubber. The crisp sky was gradually tarnished by dust and, once again, we were enveloped in a milky landscape.

Ahmet's camel hummed, as if trying to communicate with the men strapping sacks onto its flanks; it was a happy hum too, as if he liked to explore the repository of notes available to him. The white camel, on the other hand, growled, bared teeth and made a half-hearted lunge at Omar. We mounted, to walk over to the others. But my camel set off at a full gallop and, bounding along, I pushed my feet into the animal's nape, pulled the rope – attached to its nose ring – to the left, and steered it into a semicircle, before coming to a halt.

The Tubu grinned. With their daggers and swords, they presented a magnificent portrait of a bygone era. There were only a few anomalies to betray their salt road links to the twenty-first century: Omar's brown brogues, a sprinkling of dark glasses and coats that could have been plucked out of a second-hand clothes shop in London. It was a bizarre amalgam of ancient and modern.

We watched the wedding party trot into the Sahel, as a loosely formed group, and vanish into the dusty haze. As with our encampment, there was no evidence to show where they had spent the night, apart from a few charcoal flakes. Our travelling companions climbed onto their camels and, settling into the same riding positions as the day before, we rode north towards the Termit Mountains, the gangly calf trotting behind me in pursuit of its mother. From time to time, it let out a concerned mew, as if to plead it was tired.

Each person, in our cavalcade of seven, I noted, wore a turban of a different colour. Omar was in his signature dark yellow, Ahmet was swaddled in white and I wore olive. El Hadji, leading the calf's mother, wore pink, and the others were swathed in cobalt, chestnut-brown and black, respectively. I spent much of the morning on our group's flank as we rode across a denuded landscape: the sky seemed to merge into the ground, like a watercolour painting, and shafts of sunlight periodically illuminated a blurry panorama.

We passed a wandering herd of zebu and, later, Ahmet pointed out a family of Bororo, or Wodaabe, wrapped up in rugs. Rennell Rodd observed:

> The Bororoji are a darker section of the Fulani than many of the purer divisions in the south... Most of them have no permanent habitation... Their women are slender, tall and straight, with fine oval faces and straight, black hair. The Fulani believe that one day they will return to the east, whence their tradition says that they came, but how or why or when they left this unknown home has not been explained.

Bovill, however, sheds some light on this mystery:

> In the oases of the Sahara, Jewish communities long preserved their identity, but in the Sudan they were soon absorbed into the great mass of the native population among whom traces of Jewish blood may still frequently be noticed. Probably no people

of the Western Sudan contains a greater element of Jewish blood than the pastoral Fulani.

At midday we stopped, hobbled the camels and let them loose to graze. I found what looked like a dried-up pond and, in it, shards of pottery. I scanned the ground for flints, the usual signs of a Neolithic settlement but, finding none, I was unable to date the pieces. As I ran my finger over the jagged, but smoothly worn edge of a pottery fragment, I looked up and saw a white, long-eared desert fox studying me from the crest of a dune.

16

A bustard flapped clumsily into the air and banked over a vista of undulations. In the dimming light, we replenished our water at a well and camped beyond it – in the bowl of a dune. In the four hours since we stopped for lunch, we had ridden over a sandy carpet overlaid with a bedraggled tapestry of botanical threads, like old cobwebs, which were attached to spider-like plants that skittered across the surface in the wind. And tall Jurassic-looking shrubs with venous leaves appeared in clusters, and then disappeared again. Along the way, I learnt Omar had been born in 1956 and, in his telling me, there was a reflective pause, perhaps suggesting it was redundant information and had long ago been discarded as irrelevant; like Ahmet, he had no idea of his actual birth date.

The small grey radio crackled into life as night replaced dusk, and the silence was punctuated with the loquacious sentences of a French broadcaster.

'The rebels invited the Red Cross to see the hostage they kidnapped from Tanout last week,' Ahmet announced. 'They travelled into the Aïr and, apparently, the hostage is well.'

A sagacious move by the MNJ rebels, I reflected, as it demonstrated their humanity. 'When I fought,' Ahmet continued, 'in the last rebellion...'

'You fought in the rebellion?' I interjected.

'Yes,' Ahmet replied. 'Both Omar and I did.'

'I didn't know.'

'I fought with the Tuaregs in the Aïr Mountains,' he explained. 'Omar fought with the Tubu rebels on the south-east border with Chad. I remember,' Ahmet resumed, 'how safe I felt sleeping in the mountain's network of caves. And we never had to worry about water – there's always water in the caves.'

'How long did you fight for?'

'Two years,' he answered. 'Rhissa ag Boula was my commander.'

There are in the region of eight hundred thousand Tuaregs making up eight per cent of Niger's population, and they are mostly concentrated in the Aïr region: 'The Tuareg,' wrote Rennell Rodd, 'are not a tribe, but a people.' The Tuaregs, like the Tubu, do not have a country of their own. They were essentially disenfranchised when their territory was carved up by the European powers at the 1885 Berlin Conference. Today, the desert-dwelling Tuaregs mostly inhabit Niger, Algeria and Mali. Following Niger's independence their situation deteriorated, as they remained politically, economically, socially and physically isolated from the country's centre of power in Niamey. Their language, Tamashek, was banned and, with the desertification of the Sahel between 1968 and 1974, and 1984 and 1985, when much of their livestock died, many Tuaregs had to exchange their desert life for the cities where, not only impoverished, but also culturally and economically alienated, some collected in refugee camps while others emigrated to Libya and Algeria.

During the 1980s, Niger and Mali promised resettlement projects if the Tuaregs returned from Algeria and Libya, but these initiatives failed to materialise, and those who did return were met with a hostile reception. Both the Niger and Mali governments refused to help the drought-stricken Tuareg and, on 7 May 1990, the Tuaregs attacked a food warehouse at Tchin Tabaradene, about two hundred and fifty kilometres south-west of Agades. In retaliation government troops, unable to find any suspects, killed hundreds of Tuareg civilians. Niger and Mali endeavoured to play down the troubles but, by August, the European Parliament feared the 'extinction' of the Tuareg. Moussa Traoré, Mali's president, announced that the army had mastered the situation, but then, in early September, Tuaregs killed two hundred soldiers – an act which prompted Ali Sabou,

Niger's president, to call for the Tuaregs to lay down their arms. The Tuaregs, however, retorted that they were preparing for war.

As in the time of the seventeenth-century Sultan of Agades (Muhammad al-Mubarak), when the Tuareg tribes rallied against the Sultan of Bornu's invading forces, so now the rebels collected in the Aïr and entrenched themselves in the mountain strongholds of Bagzane, Adrar Tamgak and Gabon, from whence they orchestrated an effective guerrilla campaign. The Niger militia, conscripted predominantly from the plain-dwelling Songhay and Djerma, struggled in what was, for them, an alien landscape, and in response, the army laid siege to the Aïr, as if it was a medieval citadel. Despite the peace agreement, signed five years later on 24 April 1995, there continued to be hostilities until 8 June 1998 when the last rebels finally laid down their arms. However, some Tuaregs insisted that the Niger government had not fulfilled the articles of the 1995 treaty, which was one of the trigger points for the second rebellion that flared up in 2007.

Even in the autumn of 2004, when I lived in Agades, there was a night curfew and an embargo on all travel into the northern Aïr. A few days after my arrival, on a visit to the market, a military jeep was parked outside the bank and a young soldier, dressed in desert khaki, sat behind a metal tripod in the back; on the floor next to him discreetly, but immediately within reach, lay what looked like a general-purpose machine gun and hundreds of rounds of ammunition. I could not tell which Nigérien peoples the driver and his comrade belonged to, only that they were militia. They both looked uncomfortable as Tuaregs strolled past, as if oblivious to their existence. I smiled at the soldier squatting behind the tripod and the radiant, but embarrassed, grin he returned suggested he was simply pleased to be acknowledged by a pedestrian of whatever creed or colour.

'I fought in the Aïr with the Tuaregs between 1990 and 1992,' Ahmet explained, as he warmed his hands over a bed of embers. 'In the beginning we survived by eating plants and wild game, like gazelle. Then, with the arrival of Mano

Dayak, who brought jeeps, satellite phones and munitions, regular food supplies were organised from Algeria.' He prodded a glowing branch and smouldering flakes fell away like thawing rooftop snow. Then sadness crept over Ahmet's face, as if he was reliving some glum moment from his life as a rebel.

Mano Dayak was the charismatic Tuareg rebel leader who, in his mid-forties, died in a suspicious plane crash in 1995 on his way to negotiate with government officials. I had lodged in Dayak's house for the last few days of my stay in Agades. It was situated some distance from the old quarter and was, by the town's standards, a plush abode that nestled in the centre of its own expansive compound; it had a sophisticated dining-cum-sitting room, and the rarity of a bathroom. My other lodgings in the old quarter, before I decamped to Mano Dayak's house, harboured the skeleton of a Tuareg tent in a courtyard shaded by two acacias. Beside the house Agaly, a caretaker, lived in an annexe with his wife and four small children, and we often discussed the first Tuareg rebellion as we sat under a leafy canopy. He spoke French quickly – accentuated with breathy syllables – wore long white shirts over his wiry frame and walked with an earnest scurry. One of the estimated twenty thousand civilians who fled the conflict to neighbouring countries, Agaly explained he took his family to Nigeria and did not return until the peace treaty was signed. It was, apparently, not uncommon for the Niger militia to form gangs and randomly beat up Tuaregs and, at other times, be responsible for indiscriminate murders. The night-time peace of Agades was often shattered by gunfire, as rebels crept into town looking for jeeps, munitions and other accessories to steal. On one occasion, they broke into the sultan's home and, at gunpoint, insisted he swore allegiance to their cause or he and his family would be shot. But the sultan refused and the rebels left without harming anyone.

'Before the rebellion,' Ahmet continued, 'Mano Dayak had a tourist agency in Agades which employed Rhissa ag Boula. I knew them both well. Mano was a good man,' he said affectionately. 'He always made sure the wounded were evacuated to Algeria for medical treatment. We were four hundred rebels, but the government claimed we were two thousand.' As we finished eating the last strands of spaghetti, the sound of a lyre's delicate chords arose from our companions' camp. 'Mano used to say,' Ahmet mused, 'that if he was with the Tubu – he feared no one.' Despite the many cultural similarities between Tubu and Tuareg they were, up until the Tubu joined the rebellion in 1994, traditional enemies.

'Why did you feel the need to join what was then only a Tuareg rebellion?' I asked him.

'I was young and passionate,' Ahmet replied, 'but mostly I was deeply concerned and frustrated by the government's prejudices towards my people with regard to basic civil liberties like education, and other social and economic issues.' Ahmet explained how he travelled to Libya, where he made contact with Rhissa ag Boula and other Tuareg rebels and, from there, accompanied them to Djanet (in Algeria) and then down through the Aïr Mountains to Bagzane.

'I did my military training in the Azoro Mountains,' he remarked. 'There were nineteen of us Tubu and an Arab, Ahmet Mahamat Abdallah, who was our leader.'

Comets blazed through the silken blackness, trailing wakes of powdery light, and satellites glided neatly across the glistening sky.

'While chatting with Mano Dayak during the rebellion, I said: "If you are lucky, we'll make you President of the Republic. With us you'll succeed".'

17

'*Allāhu Akbar*,' Omar murmured. '*Ṣubḥāna rabbi al-'azīm*,' [Praise be to my Lord, most great]. His syllables seemed to purr, as I awoke to a chilly moonlit morning. '*Sami'a Allāhu li-man hamidahu*,' [God listens to the one who praises him]. The freezing air tickled my nostril hairs and I felt a numbing around my cheeks. '*Ṣubḥāna rabbi al-a'lā*,' [Praise be to my Lord, most high]. '*Allāhu akbar*.' The fire then crackled into life and Ahmet began to whisper his recitals. After he had finished, I reached for my leather-bound journal and, enveloped in the folds of a thick blanket, began to scribble in its creamy pages.

We left earlier than usual that morning and, as we rode further across the Sahel, the landscape became prairie-like and plants, producing tennis ball-sized fruit with watermelon-like markings, peppered the ground.

'They are,' Ahmet observed, 'poisonous to man, but edible to goats and horses.' Unlike the Sahel to the west of Agades, there were no fragments of petrified wood and, judging by the barley-brown grass knotted over the surface, it was not difficult to imagine the area as a lush paradise during the rainy season.

I felt quite at home with my companions as we travelled north-west, and the sand became increasingly littered with dung and bleached camel bones, as if carcasses had been ripped apart by scavengers.

'We left the mountains at the end of 1992,' Ahmet said, as if thinking about the previous night's conversation. 'Twelve of us went south of Nguigmi to open a front in the bush – and that led to the creation of the FDR.'

'FDR?' I inquired.

'*Front Démocratique Révolutionnaire.*'

Ahmet explained how he was deported, then elected into government in 1996 and, when Nigérien soldiers murdered one hundred and fifty Tubu refugees, he was sent as an eyewitness to the mass grave near Bosso.

'There were only two Tubu politicians at that time,' he recounted glumly. 'After I saw those bodies we met the president and I told him: "It was inhuman." The president sent me to renew contact with the rebels in the Lake Chad area, and this led to the signing of the peace agreement between the FDR and the Niger government at N'Djamena on 21 August 1997. I was one of five in the Tubu delegation that attended those meetings. Issa Lamine,' Ahmet continued, as I changed my legs from one side of the camel's neck to the other, 'was leader of the FDR. Now he is the respected Health Minister.'

'Could the Tubu and Tuareg really have their own country?' I enquired, as carefully as if fly-casting for a brown trout.

Ahmet studied me, his pupils fleetingly contracting into bayonets. 'Why not?' he challenged. 'We used to talk about it during the rebellion – with Mano and the others. What it would be like if we had our own country – and how it would work.'

'How might it work?'

'Niger would be split into two,' Ahmet replied. 'Everything east of, but including, the Aïr down to Zinder – and across to the Chad border – would be Tuareg and Tubu.'

'Would it work economically?' I quizzed. 'I mean, apart from the Aïr's uranium, are there other natural resources?'

'Oil has recently been discovered in the Manga – in the east. And there are diamonds in the Aïr.'

'That could make your country quite wealthy,' I suggested. 'And your capital: Agades?'

'Zinder,' he retorted. 'It's between the Tuareg and the Tubu.'

It was an extraordinary feeling to be on a camel discussing the conception of a new state in the twenty-first century; two nomadic peoples who wanted their own country, to protect their own kind, on their own terms.

'What do you think happened to Mano Dyak?'

'He was murdered by the government in that plane crash,' Ahmet replied. 'We lost our leader that day.' There was anger in his first sentence, and a profound regret in the second.

'And Rhissa ag Boula?'

'He is good for the nomads and their struggle,' Ahmet answered. 'The nomads need someone like him to fight for them.'

As we rode across the Sahel, the landscape transformed into a panorama of gentle undulations, like a sheet rippling in a summer breeze. A herd of gazelle sprinted out of sight into puffs of chalky dust, and two bustards lifted into the sky and flew towards a smear on the horizon that might have been an oasis.

18

'Chad rebels attacked a position ninety kilometres north of N'Djamena yesterday,' Ahmet gabbled excitedly, as he listened to the radio and scooped a spoonful of couscous. 'There are reports that the rebels entered the capital early this morning.'

'*C'est pas bon*,' Omar muttered. '*C'est pas bon.*'

'Two of the political factions against the Chad government are Tubu,' Ahmet explained. 'The problem is that if things heat up there, it could well affect things here.'

'*C'est pas bon*,' Omar persisted. '*C'est pas bon.*'

The rebels, I learnt from Ahmet, began their advance a thousand kilometres away on the eastern border with Sudan, and had moved towards N'Djamena in a column of three hundred vehicles – each containing between ten and fifteen armed men.

Like the hour hand of a clock, the sun moved past its zenith, yet seemed motionless as it hung in the powdery-white sky.

'*Al-salāmu 'alayka ayyuha al-nabī wa-raḥmat Allāh wa-barakātuh.*' [Peace be upon you, O Prophet, and the mercy and beneficence of God.] '*Al-salāmu 'alāynā wa-'alā 'ibād Allāh al-ṣāliḥin,*' [Peace be upon us and unto God's righteous servants] Omar and Ahmet prayed.

A while later, we loaded the camels and walked away from the rebellion in the south – towards the Tuareg insurgency in the north.

'Omar says we covered forty-five kilometres yesterday,' Ahmet translated, 'and that we'll probably do the same today.'

'How do you say "thank you" in Tubu?'

'*Bourgalli.*'

'Good morning?'

'*Killah-Nichirra.*'

'Goodnight?'

'*Killah-Diche.*'

'How are you?'

'*Wossara*, and the reply is *Wossou*.'

'And to command a camel to lie down?'

'*Sho, sho, sho,*' Ahmet explained, as we rode toward a flickering skyline while El Hadji's radio blared Arabian music. With Ahmet translating at my side, I learnt from El Hadji that they make the four-day trip to Nguigmi once a month, and they start to do these journeys, unaccompanied by adults, as young as eight – finding their way through the near-featureless Sahel by getting to know the wells along the way, like a dot-to-dot drawing.

* * *

When the radio whined into life that night, we learnt the rebellion had entered N'Djamena around 7 o'clock that morning. 'Rebels,' as one resident of a Western embassy told Reuters, 'are headed for the palace and are about two blocks from here.' A witness told the BBC that thirty military tanks had been set on fire and the town was under the control of the rebels. Another source confirmed that they occupied the capital's outlying neighbourhoods 'and a good part of the city centre, after intense fighting with government forces'. The rebel command announced they had the presidential palace surrounded, that the president was inside, and they planned to attack the palace later that evening. Just before dusk, however, troops attempted to recapture parts of the city, but their gains were reportedly small and it seemed – from the adrenalin-charged voice of the French broadcaster – that an uneasy calm had settled over N'Djamena with the arrival of night. '*Et la peur?*' the journalist questioned an interviewee with melodramatic sensationalism. '*Et la mort?*'

As these events were broadcast to millions of viewers around the world, the terrain we were journeying across – with rebellions due north and due south – must have looked on the television screen as if it was one of the most dangerous places on the planet, yet I was serenely happy. Although saddle- and back-sore, I was at home in the wilderness and felt safe with my Tubu companions. Comets skimmed across the night sky like skipping-stones across a glassy loch, and there was an abundance of creeping satellites, as if the entire world wanted to know what was happening around us.

'Even though the Tuaregs greatly outnumber the Tubu,' Ahmet mused, 'we are like brothers. We still talk about the concept of our own country.'

'Would it be a democracy?'

'Of course.'

'How long did Omar fight in the rebellion?'

I waited for Ahmet to translate my question, and then for Omar's answer.

'Five years,' Ahmet replied. 'Omar was one of four hundred Tubu rebels who went to ground in the bush around what was once Lake Chad. The undergrowth there is so dense, we call it a "wood" – you can hardly see your hand in front of your face.'

Omar spoke and Ahmet listened attentively.

'He says not a shot was fired until the army murdered our people but, after that, the president became scared of us. The difference between this rebellion in Chad and the one we fought in,' Ahmet continued, 'is that theirs is politically motivated – whereas we were fighting for our civil liberties.'

'Was Omar married when he fought in the rebellion?'

'Non,' Omar replied, shaking his head.

'He married soon afterwards,' Ahmet explained. 'If the rebels,' he ruminated, as if after careful analysis, 'don't take the Presidential Palace within the next twenty-four hours, their rebellion will be defeated.' As a former rebel, Ahmet's insight into the unfolding rebellion in N'Djamena was fascinating.

*   *   *

'*Allāhu Akbar,*' Omar murmured in prayer – and I awoke under a sparkling night sky. The temperature hovered around freezing, and my breath looked like a Highland mist. Ahmet coughed, began the quiet recital of his morning prayers, and the light from the fire danced about us, like sprightly wood spirits. I snugly positioned my tin mug on a nest of embers and watched the water steam, simmer and then bubble. Ahmet turned on the radio and we discovered fighting had recommenced in N'Djamena's city centre at 5 o'clock that morning. Witnesses reported a cacophony of anti-tank and automatic weapon fire.

19

The sky was white, like a duck's egg; even the sun was invisible when we mounted the camels and continued north-west across the blurring Manga. Omar headed our formation, often in avuncular-seeming conversation with one of our companions, and as the morning progressed, we swayed further across the Sahel. There is a strangely thalassic sensation to long-distance camel travel: motion, perspective, horizon, and then there are the landmarks that, however small, pass into and out of sight like shimmering Aegean islands.

Much of the straw-coloured grass we had ridden across the previous day had disappeared and been replaced by sand – not white or yellow, but a pale russet-coloured grain. We passed a couple of abandoned Tubu huts: the conical abodes were, I was told, only used during the rainy season. Later that morning, the sky became pastel blue, and we arrived at a well where a Tubu family were watering their livestock.

'Out here,' Ahmet said, turning towards me as we drew to a halt, 'water is life.'

'*Sho, sho, sho,*' I encouraged, as we drew to a halt beside the well and, with a growl and a lurch, I felt the camel's legs fold up beneath me. Omar spoke with the patriarch and arms pointed north; a direction I checked with the compass hanging around my neck.

'They have just learnt,' Ahmet explained, referring to our travelling companions, 'about a party tonight. They are going to leave us now.'

'Will we see them again?'

'Probably not.'

I watched them climb onto their camels and turn north-east, and as Omar, Ahmet and I continued north-west, I glanced back and saw the huddled group disappear into the hazy, flat scenery.

As the three of us rode through the Sahel, Ahmet talked excitedly to Omar about the rebellion in N'Djamena, as if explaining the military and political ramifications from the rebels' point of view. Not a word of French was spoken, but I knew that was the subject of Ahmet's spirited monologue. Omar listened patiently, slightly hunched in the saddle and, from time to time, grunted in polite acknowledgement; it was perhaps an insight into how little he was interested in the unfolding politics, as if he acknowledged the existence of something that needed to be recognised, but, unless it affected him directly, did not need to be followed in detail. It was plain Omar was a respected man, both now and as a former rebel, but he never volunteered any of his experiences of his life during the rebellion – and I did not want to push him.

The Sahel looked like the bottom of a protected sandy bay, sprinkled with sallow specimens of marine fauna. Mostly featureless, the panorama was scattered with the relics of half-dead bushes, and the ground was finely stitched with bleached grass: home to the tiny spiky orbs that disengaged from the parent plant, like mines from a warship, and splintered into tiny shards. The acacias disappeared and it seemed the further north we rode the more spartan in character the landscape became, and the only signs of life were a few gazelles that melted into a flickering mirage.

There was no respite from the sun as we paused for lunch, and Ahmet immediately foraged for the radio. He unfolded the antennae and we were interrupted by paragraphs of French peppered with 'N'Djamena' and '*La rébellion*'. We learnt that, since we last tuned in, evacuation of Westerners had begun and helicopters had bombed a rebel column heading towards the radio station. Armed with pickup trucks – mounted with cannons and machine guns – the rebels had engaged with tanks and soldiers in an offensive to dislodge the president from his 'heavily defended palace' in the west of the city. Ahmet translated the commentary's highlights for Omar. '*C'est pas bon*,' Omar muttered. '*C'est pas bon.*'

N'Djamena was apparently divided in half: the rebels controlled the south-west and, after government troops ran out of ammunition and abandoned their defence of the radio station, the insurgents looted the building and set it alight. There was also a report of a helicopter, in pursuit of rebels, firing a missile into the main market.

'The rebels,' Ahmet observed, after the broadcast had moved on to another topic, 'are running out of time.' In the absence of any political statement from the West, the world's politicians seemed to be waiting to see what happened next, as though watching a tide – unsure if it was advancing or retreating. The radio was turned off and Omar and Ahmet began to pray: '*Allāhumma ṣalī 'alā Muḥammadin wa-'alā āli Muḥammadin* [O God, bless Muhammad and bless the family of Muhammad],' they murmured as they knelt beside one another, '*kamā ṣalayta 'alā Ibrāhīma wa-'alā āli Ibrāhīma innaka ḥamīdun majīd* [as you have blessed Abraham and the family of Abraham, surely you are glorious and worthy of praise].'

As we loaded our camels, a Tubu in a dishevelled, ash-grey turban appeared on a chestnut pony. I sensed Ahmet and Omar were unsure of the man, as if he was asking too many questions, and I hooked the folds of the white turban over my nose, to conceal my skin's colour. I had discovered if I tied my turban to reveal only my eyes, I attracted less attention. The three of us mounted, peeled off into the wilderness and left the man behind, but his eyes appeared to follow us until we disappeared out of sight.

20

Sassai came into view as the mandarin-tinted sun slowly sank behind the horizon. The four-hour ride had taken us past a couple of Tubu villages, each consisting of about twenty narrow oval tents that, from a distance, looked like overturned fishermen's boats. What little vegetation there was had disappeared altogether; the ground had become a carpet of creamy-yellow sand and the sterile flatness was replaced with hill-like dunes. Although Ahmet checked the radio every half-hour for the latest developments in N'Djamena, we mostly travelled in silence, as Omar's extraordinary sense of direction led us through the Sahel. At last, as dusk began to cast its cloak, he pointed to a rampart-like ridge and simply said: '*Sassai*.'

'*Aliste*,' Omar beckoned, as if suggesting we tighten our formation.

'We must ride closely,' Ahmet confirmed. 'Then they can see we are travelling as a group.' As we plodded into the outskirts of the sizeable Tubu village, two adolescent boys stepped out of a tent at the settlement's periphery; they wore arm daggers and, as we pulled up and Omar started to talk to them, it felt as if their duties entailed the discreet monitoring of incomers. The exchange was brief, and they pointed, as if giving directions, along the valley floor – where the majority of tents were concentrated – and up towards the silhouette of a tent situated on the far left of the ridge.

Sassai is, by Tubu standards, a considerable community, with well over forty oval dwellings – which are constructed by stretching reed mats over a woodlouse-shaped frame; they are both smaller and narrower than a Tuareg tent. The village, I discovered, had been there for over fifty years, yet was unmarked on any map, and I later discovered that no cartographer had been into that region of the Sahel, as far as I could determine, at least since the French ceded control to the Republic in 1960.

Our camels looked as intrigued by the encampment as we were, peering from left to right as if in assessment. Omar and Ahmet thanked the boys, who were, both in demeanour and appearance, young men. I felt that if we had posed a threat they would not only have raised the alarm, but probably drawn their daggers too. We rode past tents winking with charcoal fires, and climbed the ridge's shallow incline to where we had been directed. On command, our camels lurched to the ground outside a hut constructed from branches.

'Omar has a cousin who lives here,' Ahmet explained, as the camels were unloaded and a couple of boys led them away to graze. 'Her name is Zeneba el Koligue and she has a small daughter called Binti.'

'Rather than stay in the hut,' I suggested, 'let's sleep outside.'

Omar concurred, and we spread the canvas rugs in a row on the ground. An elderly lady, Attoro, whose head was wrapped in a scarf, greeted Omar. She walked stiffly; her small frame buckled with age, but I had no idea how old she was – the climate and nomadic lifestyle are not, on the whole, kind to the human body and I've seen women in their forties look as if they are sixty. Another boy lit a fire for us and it became apparent that, as we were guests, children would attend to our chores.

From where we were perched on the ridge, we had a commanding view beneath and around us and, in the diminishing light, could watch the panorama unfurl like a seemingly endless ocean. In the misty hues near the tents, there were a few umbrella-like acacias, looking like something from an oriental watercolour. Dung beetles stumbled across the sand, and a group of children were seated in front of a hut constructed from branches and trunks.

'*Mosquée*,' Ahmet explained, following my inquisitive look. 'They are being instructed by the marabout.'

As night descended, the air was scented with the drifting fragrance of burning acacia twigs and the melody of children's laughter. Ahmet fiddled with the radio, and we discovered the rebels in N'Djamena had 'temporarily withdrawn to give civilians time to leave the city before the launch of a new offensive'. While we listened attentively, a group of elders silently emerged out of the darkness and gracefully settled around us. I heard the gentle mention of my name: '*Aliste*.' It rolled quietly off their lips as if looking for a reference point not only to the name, but also to what strange events of life had carried this white man to their home on the back of a camel, at this time, accompanied by two of their own people. We also learnt, from the broadcaster's enthusiastic babble, that the Chad government were insisting the rebels had been pushed out of the city and that the battle was over. It appeared Ahmet's prophecy of the rebels' defeat – if they failed to capture the Presidential Palace imminently – was proving perceptively accurate.

The glint of campfires flickered amidst a shroud of silhouetted tents and grazing camels. A goat was ushered over to us as if in presentation and, slightly away from our huddled group, a man pressed it to the ground, held its struggling legs as another drew a dagger and, clasping a hand over the animal's nostril and mouth, sliced its throat as easily as if cutting through a ripe pear. I turned away as the dark liquid pumped onto the sand and became a puddle-like stain. After the animal had been skinned and disembowelled, the steaming liver was cut into four and cooked on the embers beside our teapot.

As the goat meat was hacked into small pieces and put into a pot resting on a glowing bed, I was aware a deep peacefulness had settled over me. I unravelled my turban, ruffled my knotted hair and watched the firelight illuminate the bony, wizened features of the elders around us. Omar passed me a piece of liver in his hands and, thanking him, I nibbled the hot, rubbery meat. The Sahel was still and everything looked as if it had been washed and polished – from the camels to the stars, from the coral-like acacias to the beetle-like tents.

* * *

The following morning we learnt thousands of Chadians were fleeing N'Djamena, and the French, convinced of another rebel offensive, were still evacuating foreigners. But all that, and the Tuareg insurgency to the north of us, seemed a world away and I knew if we were endangered, I could not be in better company. I was travelling with former Tubu rebels through their landscape – home to one of the planet's hardiest and most resilient peoples.

'Do you know,' I enquired, 'where the Tubu came from?'

'In the time of our great-grandfathers,' Ahmet answered reflectively, '*les anciens* [the ancients] said we came from Yemen.' Omar said something, and Ahmet replied as if translating my question.

'*Yemen*,' Omar agreed, and nodded in confirmation.

Catherine Baroin, a French anthropologist who lived in Tasker on the Manga's western fringe in the early 1970s, observed:

> Little is known about the ancient history of the Tubu, but we do know the Tubu are named after the Tibesti Mountains of Northern Chad, which in local dialect are called *Tu*: Tubu translates as 'people of the *Tu*', and they are sometimes known as the Sahara's black nomads. Even in good years when rainfall is plentiful, herders must move their animals from pasture to pasture all year round. Because they have no fixed homes, most Tubu lead a nomadic life.

Today, the majority of Tubu live around the Tibesti Mountains in northern Chad and, apart from those living in eastern Niger, there are a minority in southern Libya.

The children were once again collected on the ground outside the *mosquée* in front of the marabout; the congregation of about thirty, who appeared to be aged between seven and twelve years old, were seated in a couple of ragged rows. Some held long wooden plaques inscribed with passages from the Qur'an – written with black ink in an elegant, flowing hand. The boys, like their fathers, were dressed in a colourful assortment of robes and turbans, but with the noticeable absence of arm daggers, and the few girls wore flamboyant dresses and matching scarves, like their mothers. It seemed that, as a people, the Tubu respected and enjoyed the use of vibrant colour; it was perhaps not just a mark of their own identities, but a proclamation of life within the stark landscape they inhabited.

I learnt from Ahmet that children studied the Qur'an from eight to twelve in the morning, and then from two to six. There appeared to be no other curriculum apart from that subject, and the remainder of their day was taken up with family chores and responsibilities. At a glance, nomadic life and Islam seemed a harmonious combination – one of a wilderness existence and spiritual discipline.

Beyond the ridge, where we were lodged, Ahmet and I walked to an unoccupied settlement of huts built from gnarled branches, which were lived in only during the summer months. These round, wooden structures were covered with dead branches; there was a small entrance, which you had to crouch to pass through, and the roof's apex was pointed, like a bee stinger. Ahmet wandered around with his hands clasped behind his back, and then we returned to our hut, where we found Omar had changed into a marigold-yellow robe and matching turban; framed against the sand, the suave outfit complemented his ebony-coloured skin. I did not have any replacement robes, and was becoming increasingly conscious of my grubby appearance after living and sleeping in them for five days; the state of our clothes was of no great importance when we were in the saddle or sleeping rough, but it was instructive to find just how conscious I was of the way I looked in Sassai, and how much I yearned to slip into some clean robes as a matter of social dignity.

Ahmet positioned the antennae, and the radio whirred and crackled before finding a current of undistorted French.

It seemed that a Darfur rebel group, allies of the Chad government, had raced to N'Djamena, which was why the rebels had pulled out of the city: to face the threat. In addition, the broadcaster announced that the UN Security Council had urged member states to assist the Chad government, which 'gave the go-ahead to France and other countries to help President Deby'.

'The rebels have lost,' Ahmet declared. There was no emotion in his voice – it was matter-of-fact analysis by someone who had fought in one rebellion, as he observed another. 'Even though they controlled the city,' he continued, 'they had to take the Presidential Palace. Without its capture, they would fail. They did not take it and they have failed.'

'And now?'

'The fighting will go on for a bit – then the rebellion will fizzle out,' he pondered. 'It's over.'

Peering through the hut's configuration of trunks, branches and bundles of dried grass, it was easy to observe the happenings around us. Binti's mother, Zeneba el Koligue, wandered past holding the hand of her baby son, and as she did so, presumably conscious of our presence, covered her face in the folds of a scarlet and green scarf. Binti, aged about nine, had both hands clasped around a giant wooden pestle as she pounded grain in a wooden mortar-like bowl; her dress – a vivacious collage of blue, red, pink, yellow and black patterns – billowed in time with the muffled blows. Her scarf was neatly tied over her head like a pirate's, and the tail draped between her shoulder blades. She wore a silver bangle on her right wrist and seemed contentedly at one with the performance of the task.

The radio presenter described how Mr Deby had won three elections since seizing power after a coup in 1990, and went on to explain that the legitimacy of the elections had been challenged. We also learnt that the streets of N'Djamena were littered with putrefying corpses and burnt-out vehicles, and the city was still full of the sound of automatic gunfire. The sun shimmered in a jay-blue sky and, beyond the bloated goatskin hanging beside the small arched entrance, I watched a troop of camels returning from the wilderness.

Our wicker-like hut slowly filled with a gathering of Sassai's elders, and the dialogue was mostly confined to a quiet flow of questions directed at Omar.

'The man on your left has a bad back,' Ahmet translated amid the dignified conversation, 'and he was wondering if you had any medicine?'

'What happened?' I asked.

Ahmet translated my enquiry and the elder, in a yellow robe and white turban, replied in that quietly resilient Tubu tone. 'He says he fell off a camel about a month ago – and it's been bad ever since.'

'Where does it hurt?'

Ahmet translated, and the elder pointed to his lower back.

'I might be able to offer some relief, but I am unable to cure it,' I replied. Retrieving a strip of paracetamol pills from my medical kit, I explained to Ahmet how they should be administered. I later learnt that there were only four doctors in the Manga; three of whom were based in Nguigmi, and patients had to travel hundreds of miles by camel if they wanted medical assistance.

There was, in Sassai, a preponderance of mothers in their mid-teens, as if those years were the preferred period for having a first child. Unlike Westerners, the Tubu were supportive of having children at that age, and a philosophical structure was in place to nurture and assist. The men, on the other hand, did not marry until much later and there was, I discovered, often a ten-year gap between husband and wife. A part of me envied what I saw of the Tubu community: close-knit family and generational continuity – something we in the West have perhaps lost in our pursuit of a better world. And, within that loss, we have perhaps mislaid a part of who we are.

The pauses became longer between the elders' questions and Omar's answers and, one by one, they each gracefully left. Their robes barely rustled as they got up, and they seemed to glide across the sand as they quietly disappeared out of view. Ahmet flicked on the radio, but there were no new updates about the rebellions to the north and south of us; indeed, since the battle for N'Djamena had begun, Aghaly ag Alambo and his Tuareg rebels had fallen silent – perhaps they were even grateful that the spotlight, for the moment at least, had been taken off them. I noticed a subtle shift in Omar, as if he was thinking about our impending three-hour journey from Sassai to Kossatori, and his relaxed posture swiftly left him. He stood up and began busying himself with the packing of our kit. Ahmet followed suit, as did I, and our three camels arrived, in the stewardship of a boy.

'Sho, sho, sho,' he ordered, and the animals groaned as they rocked to the ground. It was mid-afternoon. Omar talked to one of the elders, who pointed north-west, and we mounted up. My camel peered towards the horizon, as if politely asking for a steer, and we walked down the ridge's incline, past the mellifluous singing of two young women in a tangled copse and away from Sassai.

Plate 1 The Wodaabe have no concept of God: they call the sky 'Allah'. Nor do they have a word for government – as with God, they recognise it only as recognised by others.

Plate 2 The Wodaabe are aesthetes.

Plate 3 Zebu: the Wodaabe's long-horned cattle.

Plate 4 Tuareg culture: the Tuaregs are not a tribe, but a people.

Plate 5 A Zinder palace guard.

Plate 6 Nguigmi's camel market. There could be as many as a thousand dromedaries for sale on any one day.

Plate 7   Ahmet and Omar: our friendship was sealed in the wilderness.

Plate 8   Our Tubu companions for the first leg of our journey across the Manga.

Plate 9 All Tubu men, in the Manga, carry daggers, or swords

Plate 10 Tubu translates as 'people of the Tu', and they are sometimes known as the Sahara's black nomads.

Plate 11 At a Manga well: water is everything. If there's no water, the animals start to die, and then the people start to die.

Plate 12 Tubu children, living in the Manga, study the Qur'an from eight to twelve in the morning, and then from two to six.

Plate 13 Binti pounding millet.

Plate 14 One of Sassai's elders.

Plate 15 Inside a Tubu winter tent. Protected from the sun, yet illuminated by light through the miniscule holes in the pleated mats that covered the tent's woodlouse-shaped frame, the Tubu home is shady and cool.

Plate 16 Tubu belongings.

Plate 17 A Tubu summer hut.

Plate 18 View from a Tubu abode: the Tubu think about their camel's needs before their own.

Plate 19 The Aïr Mountains is a treasure trove of rock art.

Plate 20 Looking east across the Ténéré desert from the Aïr Mountains.

Plate 21 Tubu women: the role of Tubu women is to do the cooking, look after the children and attend to the herds.

Plate 22 A Fulani home: the small, igloo-shaped huts were made of thin, tight-packed branches and, from the back, resembled giant balls of garden twine that had been cut in half.

Plate 23 The Fulani believe that one day they will return to the east, whence their tradition says that they came, but how or why or when they left this unknown home has not been explained.

Plate 24 Tending to the goats.

Plate 25 Elhadji Mohamed Sali who thought all white people were French.

Plate 26 As Ahmet saw me: how I looked, in the saddle, to the Tubu, Arabs, Fulani and Kanuri.

Plate 27 Apparently founded in the mid-1800s, I was told no white person had ever visited Laraba.

Plate 28 Larabian children.

21

Like some Iron Age fort in Britain, the village of Kossatori perched on top of a vast, silhouetted dune that could be seen for miles around. As we approached it, Sassai already belonged to another archipelago. Swaying across the wilderness that afternoon, I learnt there were nine hereditary Tubu chiefs in the Manga and one of them, Mari Elhadji Chorigui, lived in Kossatori. Ahmet had not met him before and, as with the Termit Mountains which he had yet to visit, there was a sense of anticipation when he spoke of them both. He proposed a meeting with the Tubu chief. 'When there are people of importance like you travelling through,' he explained, 'it's not polite if one doesn't put in an appearance.' I had not seen myself as important at all; it seemed, rather, another acknowledgment of how long it had been since any Caucasian had passed through this region.

* * *

We slept inside a hut on the crest of a dune opposite the concentration of tents where the chief and his family lived. Dawn arrived and the sun's crescent tip appeared above the horizon. The sky turned lava-orange and the spiky, silhouetted huts resembled Ottoman battle-helmets. A fire hissed into life and the hut became softly choked with acacia-wood-scented smoke, which quickly dissipated. I absorbed that sound of incremental movement that belongs to the wilderness pre-dawn routine when, abruptly, my senses shuddered as a barrage of French splintered the peace.

The streets in N'Djamena, the broadcaster announced, were still scattered with corpses and one of the hospitals was inundated with at least a hundred injured people. The rebels had agreed a ceasefire 'because of the suffering of the Chad people'. The government, however, were dismissive, saying they had no one to sign a ceasefire with, because the rebels no longer existed as an organised group: looting was commonplace in the city centre and the rebels, by all accounts, were holding their positions on the capital's fringes, where they claimed they could easily take N'Djamena if it were not for the French soldiers. It seemed France's sphere of influence, conceived so long ago at the 1885 Berlin Conference, was alive and well – certainly from what I had seen and heard, both in Chad and in Niger.

'Are the Tubu immune to the effects of riding,' I queried, after Ahmet turned off the radio, 'if they're not used to being in the saddle?'

'No,' Ahmet replied.

'I'm pleased to hear that.'

'It's nearly a week since we left Nguigmi,' he explained, as he offered me a thimbleful of sweet tea, 'but now I'm used to it. It usually takes four or five days. Omar thinks your camel is too small for you. From today you will ride the big white camel.' I was relieved to hear it.

'Good,' I replied.

'This morning,' Ahmet announced, 'we will meet the chief, but, before then, we will visit one of the tents next to us.'

Ahmet was dressed in a lavender robe, and a pale blue turban was meticulously wrapped around his crown; the remaining material was arranged, bib-like, under his chin. As we strolled the short distance to one of the tubular tents, he explained that eighty per cent of the Tubu lived in Chad, and the remaining twenty per cent made their home in the Manga. He stood outside the burrow-like entrance of one of the tents, hands behind his back. A woman, her voice tinged with a rhythmic hum, invited us in. We crouched through the low entrance into the arched home where, beyond a reed panel between the living area and the entrance, the stooping middle-aged patriarch quietly greeted us. His mouth and nose were concealed in the folds of a white turban. His wife sat with her back propped against the low bed, her young son nestled backwards into her chest. Her daughter, in a more flamboyant crimson dress than her mother's, sat beside them, chin and mouth hidden in the patterns of a vivid scarf. Another middle-aged woman huddled in the corner and a beautiful young girl, in a coffee-coloured shawl and a dress tailored from the same cloth as her sister's, elegantly squatted, observing us with dark eyes full of discreet fascination.

A Tubu tent's framework, I discovered, was crafted from the pliable roots of some Sahelian bush which, stripped of bark, are arched into position like giant ribs; the stronger date wood is also used. At the far end was a papyrus-like screen, behind which the inhabitants could dress out of sight, and in front, a pile of carefully folded rugs were stacked above a rustic bed – the principal piece of furniture. And stowed along a tent's wall was a dilapidated black metal trunk, used for storage. About a third of the tent's space was covered with mats laid on top of a wooden grid that had been raised slightly off the sand, to create a carpeted platform. Beside the entrance, an area was set aside for cooking, and the space between domesticity and recreation seemed to be delineated by a support pole positioned, approximately, in the tent's centre. Protected from the sun, yet illuminated by light through the minuscule holes in the pleated mats that covered the tent's woodlouse-shaped frame, the Tubu home was shady and cool. From the outside it looked opaque, but it allowed the occupants a visual awareness – albeit blurred – of happenings outside.

A blackened cauldron rested on a cradle above lethargic flames and, next to it, a teapot sat in a wire basket on a nest of smouldering charcoal and chalky ash. Apart from a large pewter-coloured bowl, a contorted bucket, and a walking stick propped against the tent, there did not appear to be any other household utensils or furnishings. As we crouched near the entrance, Ahmet was dotted with flakes of light and his coal-tinted pupils glinted as we rose to leave.

We emerged under an enamel-blue sky that burned with a molten sun, and the horizon flickered as the Sahel fanned out around us. Omar was already loading the camels, and my pack was being folded away into a canvas blanket and tied onto the flank of the large white camel. We said goodbye to our lean and reserved host, Ousman Youskomi, and his obedient eleven-year old son and, mounting our camels, we steered towards the cluster of tents on the dune opposite where the chief and his family were camped. As I lurched upwards, the difference in size of the white camel from the one I had been riding was immediately noticeable, and I could feel the power in his steps and shoulder blades as he paced across the sand.

We descended one dune and began to climb another, where, close to the summit, we stopped on a curving ridge and instructed our camels to lie down. Mari Elhadji Chorigui, one of the nine hereditary Manga chiefs, emerged from a tent that was larger than the others; he was dressed in pristine white robes and a gold turban, and his bearing seemed to separate him from the other Tubu, as if he was used to being obeyed. A man in his early forties of about my height and build, he was taller than most Tubu and had a broader frame. I learnt from Ahmet that his family had been chiefs for 'a very long time' and it was apparent, in the deferential manner Ahmet adopted when being introduced to the chief by Omar, that Mari Elhadji Chorigui was a personage of some standing in the Manga. Catherine Baroin noted:

> The French presence, while good in some ways, deeply changed the Tubu way of life. The traditional role of the Tubu leader was completely undermined. Instead of leading raids, Tubu chiefs became figureheads. They were required to convey orders and collect taxes for the French. If a Tubu leader refused to co-operate, the French colonisers would choose a new chief to replace him. This caused a great deal of resentment among the Tubu.

'He was wondering,' Ahmet translated, 'if you had any medicine, as he has a cold?'

'Yes,' I replied. 'I can help a little.'

I reached for my medical kit and removed some paracetamol pills and a few sachets of Fervex: the powdered cold remedy that Dr Yovanovitch had prescribed in Niamey. I had nothing else that could offer relief and, handing the medicine to Ahmet, I explained the Fervex should be mixed with a small amount of water. The chief looked grateful and then, squinting, gazed over the spectacular panorama his ancestors had known for generations. 'It's beautiful,' I tendered. He looked at me and I felt he perhaps yearned for another sort of landscape. Yet, when the rains arrive, and the terrain erupts into a tapestry of greens it must look, from his home high up on the dune, not dissimilar to the summer's verdant steppe. He asked where we were heading and I heard, in Omar's answer, 'Termit' and 'Birnin Kazoe'; on hearing the latter, he whistled faintly, as if to highlight not only the length of our journey, but the distance we still had to travel.

Because of the authorities, we did not have the time to linger in Kossatori and I sensed in Omar a concealed anxiety about this. We had a long way to go. There was no reason to flirt with jeopardy and the possibility of being apprehended by government soldiers near the 16th parallel with an expired permit. Two Tubu and a white man would not look good, and I was sensitive to the fact that some of the material in my journal, if translated, could be misconstrued. The summary executions outside Agades, and the imprisonment of the French journalists, were still incidents of the very recent past. As we slowly rode away, Mari Elhadji Chorigui stood outside his tent, seemingly gazing after us, until he shrank to a speck on the horizon. There was a sense that he was concerned for our safety.

22

We stopped in a shallow, sandy, saucer-like depression, where a camel skeleton lay under an acacia's mottled canopy. Camel bones are an intrinsic part of the Sahel; after the flesh has been picked away by scavengers and the process of decomposition completed by ants, dung beetles and other Sahelian insects, the bones are polished by the sun with such ferocity that they attain an almost industrial whiteness and, strewn across the sand, they resemble pieces of plastic or fragments of shattered crockery.

As I plucked some hay-coloured grass and snapped a few dead twigs from a bush, the heat built around me and I hooked a turban's fold over my nose to shield my increasingly chapped mouth from the sun; I had forgotten to bring any lip salve and that oversight was causing the slow disintegration of my lips. I crouched in the sand and scooped out a hole with both hands and, making a ball of grass and twigs that I slid under a small mound of broken branches, lit a match and watched the yellow flames spread with an intense hissing sound.

While Omar unpacked a bag of couscous, unsheathed his dagger and started to peel an onion, Ahmet rolled some dough into a distorted sphere.

'I have not made bread like this,' he said, 'since making it for Rhissa ag Boula and Mano Dyak during the rebellion.'

'That was quite a long time ago,' I teased.

'We'll see,' he replied laconically.

The basic principle to baking bread in the desert is rather simple. I had seen it done in the Aïr Mountains, but it does not always work. After making the dough, a trench is dug in the sand, the bread is immersed in embers, and the hole is then filled in to form a kind of oven. The idea is that, after a period of time, the dough is unearthed and, if sufficiently baked, has transformed into a warm loaf.

As we waited for Ahmet's bread, the radio whined into life and we heard that France would (officially) intervene to protect the Chad government if called upon: 'If France must do its duty, it will do so,' was Sarkozy's reply to journalists' questions. 'Let no one doubt it.' It seemed that, although no estimates were available for the number of rebels and civilians killed, the fighting in N'Djamena had left about a thousand wounded; the streets were dotted with the 'blackened hulks of pickup trucks' and the city was virtually empty. Apparently, over twenty thousand people had fled into the neighbouring Cameroon town of Kousseri.

'Aghaly ag Alambo,' Ahmet mused, after he switched off the radio, 'must make another move soon – and quite a big one too.'

'Why's that?'

'It's been too long since the Tuareg rebels made an attack.'

'Could that be a problem?'

'There needs to be momentum,' he explained, and a reflective expression settled over his face.

Ahmet carefully unearthed the sand from around his bread and, extracting it from the ground between two sticks, he set it aside and let it cool. He tapped off the ash and sand around the crust with his dagger, revealing something that resembled a loaf, and then – after inserting an exploratory hole into its centre – he grimaced in disdain.

'C'est pas bon,' he announced irritably. 'It hasn't worked,' he continued, and winced. 'The centre has not cooked. I'll try again in a few days' time.' And the loaf disintegrated in his fingers like a failed cake.

* * *

We hoped to arrive at Iritchoui, another Tubu encampment, before dusk. I was pleased as we saddled up and rode north in the direction of the Termit Mountains: my back pain had evaporated. I had kept silent about anxieties over knife-like spasms, and I later learnt that there are few things better for an aching spine than the balanced rocking movement of being in the saddle. As the afternoon progressed, the shimmering, flat Sahel was reminiscent of a becalmed sea, and the only sign of life, apart from the camels and ourselves, was the fleeting solidarity of a few grey finches that, like dolphins, escorted us for a time and then, for no apparent reason, darted off elsewhere. We travelled across a barren landscape shaped by long, undulating valleys that looked as if they had been scooped out with a trowel. As we rode side by side across a terrain that could have belonged to the heart of any desert, we came to a small oasis where foliage and date palms clustered. Amid the crowded vegetation, a woman and two girls were busy drawing water from a well, while their black donkey, its velvety ears alertly revolving, stood patiently waiting for the order to pull.

'Beyond this well,' Ahmet explained, 'and around the corner, is the village of Iritchoui.' The camels' ears pricked to attention at the sound of splashing water, and the air smelt of warm leaves, damp sand and animal dung. As I peered into the well at the ring of rising dark water, winking like mullioned glass, Omar talked to the woman. After a short conversation, Omar explained he had just learnt that his cousin, who lived in the village, had died a few days previously. He seemed surprised at the news and thanking the woman, whose face was mostly concealed by a colourful scarf, we rode away.

'*Aliste,*' Omar beckoned.

'You must ride closer to us as we enter the village,' Ahmet insisted. 'Side by side.'

The oasis disappeared as we turned the corner and, ahead of us, surrounded by a protective ridge of dunes, was a clutch of tents dotted among a few stunted acacias. On our arrival at the encampment we were, as in Sassai, intercepted by a couple of adolescents wearing arm daggers.

'*Assalam Alaykum,*' I said.

'*Alaykum Assalam,*' they replied.

'*Wossara?*' I inquired.

'*Wossou,*' they answered.

Omar picked up the thread of introductory dialogue, and they pointed towards the community's centre.

We rode past a few tents as the sun disappeared behind the crest of a dune; goats walked and trotted between the nomadic abodes, and hobbled camels plodded in search of fodder. '*Sho, sho, sho,*' I urged and tugged the rope gently downward. Ahmet and Omar did the same, and the animals groaned as they settled outside a tent. Ousman Youskomi, a wiry man in his late thirties wearing a coiled white turban and a tan robe, greeted Omar with a warm smile. I had noticed on arriving at these encampments that Ahmet – not knowing anyone – stood beside me as if he were a stranger at a drinks party and, when introduced, betrayed his shyness by fluttering eyelids and a gently bouncing body

As the camels were led off by a boy to graze, Ahmet explained that Ousman was our host and that the tent was at our disposal. It was to be the first of several stays in Tubu tents as we progressed across the Manga. I nodded in acknowledgement and followed Ahmet inside. The interior was identical to the one we had visited in Kossatori, except that the fireplace, surrounded by a ring of loose stones, was on the right-hand side of the entrance. Omar lit a fire and Ahmet peeled back a section of roof matting beside the fireplace, so we could converse with visitors – who had already started to arrive.

The sky turned purple and Omar, Ahmet and the Tubu around us got up.

'We're going to pray now,' Ahmet announced and, as they walked off in a tight group, I noticed that, for the first time since we had arrived in Iritchoui, Ahmet was relaxing. The mostly adult males collected in prayer not far from where I was seated, and turned towards Mecca.

'*Allāhu Akbar... Allāhu Akbar,*' the aged marabout chanted. '*Allāhu Akbar... Allāhu Akbar*' and the words sailed through the dusk like a healing incantation. '*Al-taḥiyyātu li-llāhi wa'l-ṣalātu wa'l-ṭayyibātu* [Good wishes, prayers and blessings are due to God].' The evening's shroud of volcanic orange gradually dissolved into blackness, and prayers drew to a close: '*Ashhadu anna lā ilāha ilā Allāh* [I bear witness that there is no God but God],', he continued, '*Wa-ashhadu anna Muḥammadan 'abduhu wa-rasūluh* [and that Muhammad is His servant and His messenger]'.

The small congregation slowly dispersed and, as Ahmet returned with them, it was as if he was conversing with lifelong friends.

23

Omar returned with Malam Boukar, the marabout, who was dressed in flowing white from crown to ankles, and seemed almost to glow in the darkness. As they sat outside our tent, the spluttering fire illuminated the old man's puckered face: the flickering light revealed a person deeply at peace with life. His words exuded serenity and, framed against the stars around him, he seemed to be gently discussing the manner of the death of Omar's cousin. Omar – head slightly tilted to one side – looked relaxed while he listened to the marabout.

Fires glinted all around Iritchoui. In the space between our tent and another from which a chorus of convivial female voices resounded, a goat had its neck slit by two men. It was too dim to see the blood, but not dark enough to conceal the animal's legs struggling, and then falling limp. And the women's cascading chatter rose a few octaves as children, running in and out, decorated the tent with moving silhouettes.

As we sat outside, the shadows of camels roamed beyond the tents that hugged the ground like rock pool barnacles and, from time to time, the peaceful tones of Tubu would be interrupted by the moan of an invisible camel. Segments of the goat's innards sizzled on glowing embers around Ahmet's red teapot, and our tent, both inside and out, was alive with the flurry of nomadic voices keen to catch up with the latest gossip from Sassai and Nguigmi, and to hear news of the rebellions in the south and north.

Omar handed me two steaming pieces of liver. After conspicuously nibbling one of them, I discreetly scraped a hole in the sand beside me and buried the mangled lumps, being careful not to inter any bumbling dung beetles. Our tent became a hub of activity as men wandered over and, with several of them sitting around me, I felt a sense of peaceful exhilaration as I listened to their calm and soothing dialogue. Ahmet distributed thimblefuls of tea and a veiled woman – emerging out of the dark like a gliding phantom – untied the neck of a goatskin she was carrying and elegantly poured the warm, sweetened camel's milk into a large bowl, as the chattering voices continued under a mist of galaxies.

24

'As we left Iritchoui this morning,' Ahmet said, 'they commented on how at home you look on a camel.'

I smiled, as we rode across a Sahel littered with a more than usual amount of bones. It had only been an hour since we had crawled, like crabs seeking refuge in a rocky cleft, under a thorny bush to escape a belligerent midday sun. 'French military officials in Chad,' the radio broadcaster recounted, 'say the rebels are far from N'Djamena and all is quiet on the city streets.' Ahmet's prophecy that the Chad rebellion would fail had been acute: the rebels' inability to capture the Presidential Palace within a certain time frame was their downfall. 'The rotting corpses are being removed, but the city is still littered with evidence of the previous day's gun battles,' the broadcaster continued. 'At least four leading opposition figures have been arrested.' Ahmet listened – his face a mask of stern concentration – as the bulletins explained how Amnesty International were concerned that the arrested opposition leaders were at risk of either 'disappearing' or being tortured. The witch-hunt, it seemed, had begun.

'Rhissa ag Boula was on the radio this morning,' Ahmet observed, as he rode alongside me. 'I didn't catch it all, but he was saying something about the Aïr and its uranium deposits.'

The climate was changing my body: my hands were becoming leathery and caramel-coloured, and it would only be a matter of days before the Tubu began to mistake me for an Arab. As the heat increased, so did the number of flies – a genus that seems to have mastered the art of desert travel. En masse, they attached themselves, like lampreys, to our backs and then enthusiastically disengaged when we stopped – to descend on our food and water.

'How often do the Tubu move?' I asked, as we rode past a family standing around the skeletal structure of a tent.

'Whenever they have to find more grass for their herds,' he answered. 'It looks as if they arrived last night.'

It seemed, as these nomads were demonstrating, that many of the encampments were set up on a dune's crest: the Tubu appeared to favour elevation. This family had raised their tent not far from a traditional well, about thirty metres deep, that had been sunk into the hollow of a basin studded with scrub acacia; indeed, I was beginning to identify the telltale signs of where to find water and it seemed that, beneath the Manga, there was a significant reservoir.

Later that afternoon we came across an Arab cameleer, but the greetings between him, Omar and Ahmet were noticeably perfunctory and aloof. And it was then that I began to understand the Manga Tubu were like one big family. Different racial groups inhabited the same landscape, but the Arab had failed to conceal a glint of suspicion, though that might have been linked to thoughts about a white man heading north with a couple of Tubu towards the Tuareg rebellion.

'It is always like that when meeting Arabs in the Manga,' Ahmet remarked, as we turned away towards a dune's steep incline. 'In town, however, it's quite different – they are all smiles and charm.'

His observation reminded me of the Arabs I had seen and met at the camel market in Ngugimi where, because of their smaller stature, different skin pigment and bone structure, they were easy to identify; certainly the Tubu respected the Arabs as excellent camel breeders – and we were travelling through the Sahara's camel nursery. I had lost track of all the calves we had passed since beginning our journey across the Manga. It was the season.

'The Arabs favour this particular region,' Ahmet explained. 'The grass here is particularly good for camels. In Tubu this type of grass is called *Taour*.'

How clever of the Arabs, I thought, to have chosen this patch. I peered down at the skimpy veil of wispy, barley-coloured grass that loosely covered the ground like the thinning hairs on an octogenarian's scalp.

'In three months,' Ahmet continued, 'all the grass here will have been eaten, and nothing but sand will remain.'

I had heard, during the first rebellion, of Tuaregs killing an Arab and cutting out his tongue for being in the pay of the Niger government; in revenge, a band of Arabs disguised themselves as Tuaregs, in an attempt to manipulate hostilities, and attacked the Wodaabe – who did take up arms, but only as a matter of defence and no reciprocal attacks were organised. And I never heard of any conflicts between Arab and Tubu. Apart from the Aïr Mountains and its environs, the Tuareg nomads also live in the Damergou, on the Manga's western fringe – a region the authorities in Niamey had specified as out of bounds because of the ongoing rebellion. We were already well north of Tanout where, just over two weeks previously, rebels had attacked that town and kidnapped its prefect. Yet I felt no uneasiness or fear, as we continued north.

Perhaps, like Omar, I recognised the troubles as something which needed to be recognised, but, unless we were affected, they could be seen as belonging to a different realm. I was also very comfortable with Ahmet and Omar's abilities and, more importantly, the relationship that was developing between us as our journey unfolded.

* * *

The following day, after a cold night under the stars, we embarked across a landscape reminiscent of oceanic swells. A herd of gazelles evaporated in a few puffs of dust and, for a moment, there was a ruffling of leaves in a rare breeze. The horizon conjured up fictitious lakes, and a giant sun dominated the hazy blue sky, as we rode noiselessly across the silent landscape. Our camels, their large heads inching from left to right and back again, carefully kept lookout for us.

We stopped at a well, crowded with animals, to replenish our diminishing supply of water. A couple of cameleers were struggling to keep control of two fighting bulls as the animals lunged, teeth bared, at each other's faces and necks; their ugly, grey tongues lolled from jaws splattered with saliva like sea foam. As the bulls fought, camels, goats and donkeys quietly drank, seemingly oblivious to the battle around them.

'Ahmet,' I said, not wanting to appear overbearing as I watched him fill one of our water bags from a container plucked from among a throng of thirsty camels, 'I don't think we should fill up from there. We should,' I persisted, 'do it directly from the water being drawn from the well.'

'We Tubu are used to it,' he retorted.

Maybe, I thought, but I was not and did not want to fall sick. After a brief pause, I watched him pour the possibly contaminated water into the sand. I walked over to help, and we started again.

As we peeled away from the well and climbed to the crest of a ridge overlooking the basin, we found a cluster of Tubu tents where three aged men, giving an impression of vulnerability, stood outside an entrance.

'*Assalam Alaykum.*'

'*Alaykum Assalam.*'

'*Wossara?*'

'*Wossou.*'

'Inside,' Ahmet translated, in-between talking to the old men, 'their father is very sick. He is a hundred and twenty.'

'A hundred and twenty?' I repeated, checking I hadn't misheard.

'Yes. I have confirmed his age with them. Have you got any medicine left?'

I extracted the last three sachets of Fervex and a strip of paracetamol. It was all I could do to help, but his sons looked grateful as I handed them over. From where Ahmet and I were sitting high up on our camels outside the tent, I could hear a laboured throat rattling from within, as if the man's soul was holding on to the last threads of life; it is not the sort of noise that can be misconstrued. If he had indeed reached the age they suggested, he was born in the same year as T.E. Lawrence – when Lord Salisbury was Prime Minister. When he arrived in this world, it had only been three years since Gordon of Khartoum's murder and the signing of the Berlin Conference, and only thirty-three years had elapsed since Henry Barth travelled through Nguigmi on his return to Europe. In 1888, when his first baby cry was heard, Queen Victoria had thirteen years left on the throne and Winston Churchill was just fourteen years old. The strained, wheezing gasps I heard were just possibly the last living link to a pre-colonial Africa, still unblemished by the white man's carving out of territories.

This might seem a bit far-fetched: how on earth can some of these nomads reach such a venerable age without the benefits of the allegedly healthier modern world? A week later, I found solid supporting evidence for this extraordinary lifespan. We were staying with a seventy-one-year-old Tubu, Elhadji Mohamed Sali, who as a small boy then living in the Termit Mountains, remembered this same man as already being *un grand* – which loosely translates as a 'seasoned adult'.

Omar mounted his camel and, turning away from the strained, rattling breathing, we continued north. And as we went, for some unexplainable reason, I felt a momentary sadness.

25

It would take the next twenty-four hours to cross the vast valley floor, which unfurled in front of us like a seascape. We should have been able to make out the Termit Mountains' skyline ahead of us but, apart from one fleeting glimpse of a faint, lofty silhouette, they were hidden in an impermeable haze. I reached for the water bottle hidden in my knapsack, under a camel blanket, where I stored it to keep the water cool from the night before. As I surveyed the rippling panorama from the ridge where we had stopped, I filled the battered tin mug and, clasping my palms around its briefly refrigerated sides, I slowly gulped the cool liquid in a land beleaguered by pugnacious heat. If someone had offered me a chilled glass of Dom Perignon instead of what I was drinking, I would have turned it down rather than forgo the wonders of tasting, and feeling, cold filtered water under a sultry desert sun in the shade of a lone acacia. It is the finest drink in the world. My water bottle held just enough for a solitary mug, which meant only one frigid drink a day, but each lunchtime I looked forward to that simple experience as one of a lifetime's sensational highlights.

*   *   *

That evening, the sun was a luminous orange, like the beak of a yearling blackbird, as it sank into the darkening desert with an almost alarming haste. It made me wonder why, during the day, it often seemed to be an age before it budged at all.

I marvelled at Omar's ability to hold a bearing – without a compass – in a terrain bereft of any notable landmarks; it was as if he acquired a general sense of direction from the nomads we encountered along the way and then, allowing for the shifting course of our route, had somehow devised a navigational technique of his own that would perhaps have made ancient seafarers grudgingly envious.

* * *

The following morning, we rode towards the mountains, again obscured in a milky blur; our faces hidden in the tightly wrapped folds of our turbans, as gusting wind fumbled robes and dusted them with sand. We had arrived at the tidemark between the Sahel and the Sahara: there were no wisps of grass and very few acacia leaves for the camels to nibble. Unlike the Tuaregs, who use camels to carry grass when crossing the desert, the Tubu, when travelling, graze their camels on what is available as they cross the Sahel. Without doubt our three camels had lost weight, as was perhaps to be expected when travelling for eight to nine hours a day, but the Manga provided enough fodder to keep them in a healthy state and, as Ahmet had pointed out at the market in Nguigmi, 'The Tubu think about the stomachs of their camels before their own.'

Francis Rennell Rodd, the anthropologist, did not penetrate the Manga, but he did make a brief visit to the northern reaches of the Termit Mountains, after approaching them from the west – across the Damergou. As he observed, nearly eighty years previously:

> Under ordinary conditions, the mountains of Termit are visible for some time before they are reached; in point of fact on our way south we saw the Centre Peak at a distance of no less than fourteen hours marching. Approaching it, however, the intense heat and wind had obscured everything in a dense mist which limited maximum visibility to under two miles.

Not much, it seemed, had changed. Rennell Rodd continued:

> While the Tuareg and the Tebu (Tubu) live side by side with the Kanuri, the first two are such uncompromising enemies that they never adventure themselves into each other's territory. The dividing line between them is sharp and clearly defined; it runs just west of the village of Bultum, which is the last permanent settlement on the caravan road from Damagrim to Kawar by the wells of Termit, where twice a year pass caravans to fetch salt in the east. They leave in the same season when the people of the Aïr, whom they join at Fashi, also cross the desert.

That geographical demarcation between Tubu and Tuareg is, as our journey across the Manga was revealing, still very much in place. All that is missing is the ancient feuding. It is perhaps interesting – as Ahmet is living testimony – that it took the amalgam of the 1885 Berlin Conference and late twentieth-century domestic politics not only to smooth the relationship between the Tuaregs and the Tubu, but also to unite them as comrades in arms. First the French, then subsequent governments in Niamey, had tried to break the spirit of these two formidable nomadic peoples – and had failed. It was as if these nomads and the land had become one, and an entity that could not be crushed.

We were just south of the 16th parallel where, to the north-east across the Ténéré desert, Aghaly ag Alambo and his Tuareg followers were conducting their rebellion from some network of caves beneath the towering mountain of Adrar Tamgak – perhaps, even at that moment, engaging in some hypothetical debate about having a country of their own. The wounds created by the Berlin Conference's cartographical blueprint were, it seemed, as bloody, raw and unhealed today as they had been a century ago.

As we approached the foot of the Termit Mountains, which curled away northwards into the desert, we passed some abandoned branch huts that Ahmet explained 'were only occupied in the rainy season'. I remembered, when living in Agades, hearing that these mountains were sometimes used as a hideout for bandits, who, like the Barbary corsairs, menaced traffic crossing the Ténéré on the way up to the North African littoral from East Africa – a notorious smuggling route. The sporadic, but continuous passage of dilapidated trucks trundling along the rickety track between Bilma and Agades, where passengers huddled beside goats on piles of sacks eight metres high, was an important artery for trafficking anything, from counterfeit cigarettes and munitions to slaves. The Old Salt Road it appeared, yet again, was alive and flourishing in the twenty-first century.

Despite the global illegitimacy of slavery, the repugnant trade has survived: the trafficking of slaves, according to the UN, is worth an estimated $32 billion a year, and there are at least twelve million people currently in bondage around the world. In Niger alone, it has been reported that there are around forty thousand slaves. However, in October 2008, a twenty-four-year-old Ms Hadijatou Mani – who was sold into slavery when she was twelve – won a landmark case against the Niger government for failing to protect her and was awarded CFA ten million, the equivalent of £12,400, which is a great deal of money if you are a Nigérien.

The Termit Mountains, with their volcanic rocks heaped like coal spoil, and orange sand lapping against the mountains' base, are very similar in character to the Aïr. Rennell Rodd wrote:

The first description of Aïr and its people in any detail was brought back to Europe by Barth after his memorable journey from the Mediterranean to the Sudan, on which he set out in 1849 with Richardson and Overweg, but from which he alone returned alive more than five years later. Prior to this journey there are certain references in Ibn Battuta and Leo Africanus, but they do not give us much information either on the country or the people. From Ibn Battuta's description, the country he traversed is recognisable, but the information is meagre. The account of Leo Africanus, written in the sixteenth century is little better... He states that the country is inhabited by the Targa people and, as he mentions Agades, it has evidently by then been founded, but beyond these facts his description is wholly inadequate.

Targa is marked on Ortelius' 1570 *Africae Tabula Nova*, and in Joan Blaeu's 1665 *Atlas Maior* it is honoured with two inclusions: Targa and Targa reg, as if depicting a country. Rodd continued:

> According to Leo in the interior of Libya there was a people who wore the litham or veil... The third area was inhabited by the Targa. It commences from the desert steppe west of Aïr and extends eastwards towards the desert of Igidi. North-west it borders on the Tuat, Guorara and Mzab countries, while in the south it terminates in the wilderness around Agades and Lower Aïr. The boundaries of this area are quite clear: they include the massifs of Aïr and Ahagaar and the deserts immediately east and west of the former.

A photograph of Rennell Rodd in *People of the Veil*, his account of the time he spent with the Aïr Tuareg in 1922, portrays a lean, bearded man standing beside a Tuareg armed with a spear and, in another shot, he is pictured sitting cross-legged, dressing a Tuareg's wound.

*   *   *

I remembered the Aïr as a realm in its own right: mountains of serrated peaks rising out of the desert and vibrant oasis villages; puddles of life populated with pastoral Tuaregs and their herds, where children attended to donkeys and camels as chattering well water rushed along the wooden network of troughs to crops of tomatoes and cucumbers dotted among a patchwork of thorny bushes and lush flora. I had only known the landscape briefly – and it was over three years since I had passed through it on the way back to Agades.

At that time I was travelling with two Tuaregs, one of whom, Abdallah, I learnt on my return to Agades, had fought in the first rebellion.

'*ll est un vrai brave*,' Agaly had explained to me in Agades as we sat in the dappled courtyard. 'After returning to Agades with the other rebels at the government's invitation to cease hostilities,' Agaly continued, 'Abdallah visited his parents' village in the mountains, but soldiers were waiting inside their home. He walked straight into the trap. There was an extended silence before he slowly raised his AK47 and quietly said: "I'll kill you all before I go." He was totally outnumbered, yet they backed down and left. *Un vrai brave.*'

But I did not know this side of Abdallah as we crossed the Ténéré together in search of petroglyphic sites dotted along the Aïr's eastern fringe. I only knew he was married and a father of two small children. As we sat beside a fire under the stars in the mouth of a wadi studded with Neolithic impressions of giraffes, ostriches, gazelle, wildebeest, elephants and man – portraits of a vanished world when the Ténéré had been a fertile savannah – the mountainous silhouettes climbed into the night around us.

'Are there still *"Les anciens"* in Britain?' Abdallah asked.

'Who do you mean by *"Les anciens"*?' I enquired.

'Those who live in the bush and desert.'

'No,' I answered. 'There are not.'

'*Les anciens* say the dinosaurs lived in the water, and that's why they can only be found in the desert, which used to be the sea. They also say the trees were all made of stone, like the ones we find in the desert. Were there people at the time of the dinosaurs?'

'The dinosaurs disappeared sixty-five million years ago,' I explained respectfully. 'People have been around for, at most, four hundred thousand years.'

'So,' he pondered logically, 'that's why there are no rock drawings of dinosaurs.'

'Exactly.'

'Ahhhh,' he sighed, before adding incongruously: 'I think Kerry should be president.'

'Why do you think that?'

'I have listened to the radio and think Kerry is the better man. I have heard he might not have done some good things in Vietnam, but I don't think Bush and Blair are good people.'

As I peered into the Ténéré, I mentioned that I'd spent some time in China's Taklamakan desert.

'How can there be a desert in China when we hear on the radio that it's overpopulated?'

I explained that much of the population lived in the central and eastern regions, and it was the cities that were overcrowded.

'Cars?'

'Cars and bicycles,' I replied. 'The Taklamakan is larger than Niger and fits into just one of China's provinces.'

'Then why don't people in the cities go and live in the desert and bush?'

'I don't know. Maybe they have forgotten how.'

'Ahhhh,' he sighed again, and craned his neck towards a sky streaked with a flurry of comets. 'Falling stars,' he continued, 'yet they do not diminish.'

'Why do you call them falling stars?'

'It's what my parents called them when I grew up in the mountains.'

Only a few days before that conversation, Mohamed ag Boula, in retaliation for his brother's imprisonment, had attacked a military patrol and taken several hostages in the vicinity of Adrar Tamgak – just a hundred kilometres north-west of where we then were.

The following day, on a ridge overlooking the wadi of Anakom, alone and hidden away from the main concentration of rock art, I discovered that the face of a boulder had been surgically cut away, by some sort of chainsaw, to remove whatever Neolithic image had been cut into it thousands of years ago. After examining so many carefully carved images, I felt a sense of desecration on seeing this rock, which looked as if it had been decapitated. It was only on my return to Britain that I learnt how some Europeans plundered the Sahara's prehistoric repository – of everything from Neolithic tools to dinosaur skulls – and smuggled them into the EU as 'geological samples'. Indeed, around that time, a group of Germans were arrested in the Algerian Sahara after soldiers discovered a hoard of Stone Age and Cretaceous specimens in the back of their truck.

*　*　*

'Did you know a Tuareg called Abdallah when you were with the rebels in the Aïr?' I asked Ahmet, in the shadow of the Termit Mountains.

'What was his full name?'

'I can't remember.'

'I knew an Abdallah who fought with us,' he reflected. 'He was good at playing the lyre. Why?'

'I travelled with someone of that name three years ago when we visited the Aïr's rock-art sites. I only know he fought in the rebellion, but I don't think he played the lyre.'

26

We had arrived at Termit's abandoned outpost of graffiti-covered buildings, which had apparently once been used for oil exploration. The heat glared and my tongue intermittently touched bleeding lips: I was eager for the day's one dose of chilled water. The small runway – built for light aircraft – was riddled with lumpy cracks and tentacle-like vegetation. They were the first buildings we had seen since leaving Nguigmi, and they looked as if they had been deserted for at least a decade. 'They were built,' Ahmet explained, 'in the time of the last president.'

Lunch beckoned, so we settled away from the decaying premises – in the narrow mouth of a thin, snaking gorge that led up into the mountains. A young Tubu girl darted between the tangled bushes around us, singing an eerie, unsettling tune.

'*Elle est folle*,' Ahmet observed. 'Mad. She belongs to that family at the well we passed, by the buildings.'

My scalp itched and my hair was a mat of knots and congealed dead flies that, along the way, had been crushed beneath the turban by my irritated hand. It did not conjure an attractive image. 'I have to wash my hair,' I explained to Ahmet, undoing the folds of my turban. I splashed water over my crown and smothered it in apple-smelling shampoo. As I tilted my head forward, Ahmet poured a flow of water over it. I was unable to contain a murmur of relief, as the foaming liquid slopped onto the sand around me. It was one of the finest hair washes I had ever experienced; my head felt clean and the itching evaporated. I wandered up into the mountains and, finding a knoll, gazed over the immense desert panorama we would shortly be crossing.

* * *

For the first time since leaving Ngugimi we turned south and away from Aghaly ag Alambo and the rebellion. I felt a sense of relief even from Ahmet and Omar. We couldn't hang around Termit; there was little for our camels to eat and, as I understood, we had a stretch of desert to cross before we arrived at a reliable pocket of camel grass. The orange sand turned to yellow as the Termit's craggy outline receded into a blurry haze. Ahead of us, a herd of camels came into view. As we approached, we noticed one of them had just given birth and her wet calf was struggling to get up beside a bloody puddle of afterbirth. A Tubu, wearing a yellow turban on the verge of unravelling, nursed it with some milk as his small son, perched high up on the saddle of a camel, surveyed both the scene beneath him and our emergence out of the shimmering wilderness. I watched the calf gingerly wobble to its feet, as if it knew its life depended on it; shivers rippled across its body while the mother reassuringly licked its neck.

'The cameleer has invited us to camp with him this evening,' Ahmet translated. 'So we will travel with this caravan.'

'What about the calf?' I asked, watching the camels plod south in one long extended line.

'The mother will stay with the calf and then, when it's able to walk, they will find the herd later.'

'How do they do that?'

'They just know.'

We tagged alongside Elhadji Issouf's caravan and – in rhythm with the thirty-odd camels stretched out in front of us – we swayed across a landscape bathed in the shades of a late afternoon sun. Turning around, I watched the vulnerable-looking camel and her calf become smaller and smaller until, blotted out by a dune, they disappeared.

Twice that day the Tubu mistook me for an Arab, both before and after Termit. I was no longer easily recognisable as a white man and felt strangely comforted by this. I had not looked at my reflection for almost a fortnight, but judging from the backs of my hands – their texture and colour – I had some idea of how I might have appeared, partly obscured in a white turban. As we rode south, our caravan became a string of silhouettes in the glare of a sinking white sun. Many of the camels were pregnant and others walked with calves tucked in behind them, while one mother, calf at her side, drifted along the column's westerly flank, in step but aloof from the main body. I did not discover how the camel spearheading our group knew where it was going or why we were all happy to follow its lead as we humans picked up the rear, but the arrangement seemed to work as we headed south.

*   *   *

When the radio crackled into life the following morning, we learnt that Rhissa ag Boula had publicly announced his support for the Tuareg rebellion. He had, apparently, been interviewed in Paris, where he appeared to be living in exile, but apart from that there was no other news of the insurgency. It seemed Aghaly ag Alambo and his rebels had gone to ground and were, at least for the time being, content to sit it out. They knew time was on their side and were, after all, comfortably ensconced in the Aïr Mountains – a region the size of Switzerland. Chad had also disappeared from the world's airwaves as if, now the carnage was over, it could be seen as just another country in landlocked Africa.

A small flock of chirping grey finches flittered among the twisted dead branches above where we were camped, which brought to mind the March 1945 jottings of Captain Agramenko, the Russian playwright: 'Birds are singing. Buds are opening. Nature does not care about the war.' As dawn's cerulean shades heralded the beginning of another day, the camels picked up from where they had left off the night before and began to sigh and groan. Elhadji's wife wandered over with a dish of beans and goat meat, to where her husband was already huddled over our fire in quiet conversation with Omar.

The faded outline of the Termit Mountains squiggled along the horizon but, by the time we had saddled up, they had disappeared in a sea-like fog that had crept upon us. Yet this did not bother Omar. He calmly navigated through the obscure surroundings until gradually we saw the re-emergence of isolated acacias and wispy bleached grass. Then, out of the impenetrable mist, a Tubu cameleer appeared. His turban and robes were black as a coal tit's crown, and his sword was easily visible on the camel's flank. As we drew up alongside, his face remained hidden and, while Omar asked directions, his furtive eyes swivelled towards me as if in assessment. A few minutes later he was swallowed up in the fog, as he continued north.

It was eerily quiet and still that afternoon, as if we were riding through a place that knew something we did not. We saw no sign of life, and the only evidences of humanity, apart from us, were the telltale signs of a recently vacated Tubu camp – not that there was any rubbish, but the sand had been disturbed and there was some dung and string-like strips of bark: almost enough information to picture the number of tents, people and livestock that had encamped there. It was, in short, a landscape that teased the mind with the trickery of uncertainty.

27

Two days later we arrived at Tororonga. We had passed wandering camels and listened to the ghostly whining of jackals as we slept under a crescent moon. The landscape was changing into a different sort of Sahel: the undulations and basins were becoming bigger and, at times, were tinged with a lichen-green sheen. The few nomads we encountered, when asked about Tororonga, laconically observed: 'It is that way,' or 'It is far,' or 'It is beyond that hill.' A scattered chorus of bird-song replaced the silent dusks, and the setting sun was our compass as we rode towards evening horizons. Omar guided us across an unmarked terrain, and his extraordinary eyes could spot some distant cameleer when all I saw was a bush or an unidentifiable blur. Approaching Tororonga was like arriving at some rustic marina after an extended sea crossing, and the gradual approach allowed the traveller to assess his destination from different perspectives; even the sway of the camel was oceanic, like a pumice stone floating on the crest of gently lapping waves.

Tororonga was actually marked on my *Institut Géographique National* map and, surrounded by a pale yellow area indicated as a *Région Désertique*, situated just north of the freckled blue *Zone Humide*. The legend described it as a village that had wells. We rode over to the settlement's western periphery where, on a ridge, Omar introduced us to Kormay, another cousin, who was dressed in a variegated collage of colour; she greeted us with smiles and chirpy banter before settling us into a tent near her hut. It was mid-morning and, for the first time since Sassai, we were to have half a day's rest. We needed it. The accumulated fatigue of our journey – and its pace – in recent days had been such that each of us had slumped into a deep, consuming sleep after lunch. In the last two days alone we had travelled, according to the map, at least a hundred kilometres, but with all the twists, turns, ups and downs of our route, it was much more. As we lit a fire in the corner of our tent, four men arrived in an assortment of robes and turbans:

'*Assalam Alaykum.*'

'*Alaykum Assalam.*'

'How are you?'

'How is your family?'

'How are your children?'

'How is your health?'

'And the heat?'

They gracefully seated themselves around us while Ahmet brewed some Chinese tea. I lay on my side at the back of the tent, opened my leather-bound diary and began to scribble a new entry:

> 'The role of Tubu women,' I penned, 'is to do the cooking, look after the children and their homes, and attend to the herds. It is customary here, when a group of men are gathered in one of the tents, that the women do not enter but, standing outside, they collectively run through the formality of greetings while the men, seated out of sight inside, reply (also collectively) to each question in turn – this can happen at any time. Equally, it seems, the men do not intrude on a female gathering, however small.'

'If the women look after the home,' I asked Ahmet, 'the cooking, the children and the herds – what do the men do?'

'It is our role,' he replied with a smile, 'to find stray animals.'

'And?'

'To find money.'

I wanted to discover more about the Tubu women, but I was not in a position simply to wander over to them or go into their tents – nor was it ever suggested that I was permitted to do this. To have done so, I felt, would have been a serious breach of etiquette, so I never caught a glimpse of Tubu life from the female perspective. In addition, I sometimes felt frustrated with Ahmet. He was not good at giving a direct answer, and his French was heavily accented with a nasal twang so, for example, *grade* (rank) became *grotte* (cave) and *j'ai dit* (I said) sounded like *Jeudi* (Thursday), and there were long rolling *rrrrrr*'s that hovered without pause until they found the next word. He often spoke so fast that it was difficult to dissect the sentences, and I sensed my questions about Tubu culture sometimes irritated him.

However, Catherine Baroin has an explanation:

> The father eats with other adult men including neighbours and guests. They eat from a common bowl. His sons are not allowed to share his meal before they become full adults, that is, not before they are about thirty years old. Daughters eat with their mothers from a young age. There is more intimacy and less formality between them than between father and son. Husband and wife, and men and women in general never eat together; this is strictly prohibited. A husband never eats in the presence of his wife, although a wife may eat when her husband is around. However, after about three years of marriage, a married couple may start drinking tea together. For the wife, tea drinking is a relatively new habit. Young girls are not allowed to drink tea. Only after marriage, may they begin to drink tea with other people of similar age... The Tubu prefer to eat discreetly... People usually eat silently. It is a mistake to start saying something that comes directly to mind while eating.

Baroin goes on to explain that boys are circumcised around the time they reach puberty and that:

> Most Tubu girls marry between fifteen and twenty years of age. Men marry much later, usually between twenty-five and thirty. According to Muslim tradition, a baby is given a Muslim name and its head is shaved seven days after it's born. Young children, both boys and girls, keep their heads shaved for several years. They are completely bald except for a crest, a strip of hair

that runs from the tip of the forehead to the nape of the neck. Depending on family habits, children may also have one or a few tufts of hair on the top and sides of their heads... Today all Tubu are Muslims. Because the introduction of Islam was a very slow and irregular process, a precise date for its introduction is difficult to give. The religion spread to the different Tubu social groups at different speeds and times. This process took many years throughout the 1800s... Although the Tubu say their prayers in Arabic, few Tubu actually speak Arabic.

Our guests left a while later, updated with all the latest bulletins from across the Manga. Then, in the pool-like shade of our tent, Ahmet and I slipped into a conversation about Islamic daily ritual and how travelling Muslims recited a truncated version of their daily prayers.

'Do you know about Buddhism?' I enquired.

'What's that?'

'A religious philosophy – like Islam and Christianity – it's meditative and teaches compassion and that we should not hate or be greedy.'

Ahmet nodded in philosophical recognition. 'Do you say prayers?' he asked.

'I sometimes do Qi Gong,' I replied. 'I've been practising it every day in Niger.'

'What's that?'

'It's a form of physical meditation – it achieves a conscious state of absolute stillness.' Ahmet looked silently pleased as if, up until that point, he had believed I was missing something.

28

An elderly, one-eyed Tubu, his face furrowed with wrinkles, hobbled over to our fire with steps that betrayed a painful back. He stood there for a moment, stooping over us, while I surrendered my blanket and made a comfortable support for him to lean against.

'Goats die quicker when others do it,' Ahmet confessed beside me, and certainly the one whose throat he had slit an hour earlier kicked around longer than usual, but there was an endearing trace of guilt in his tone, as if it was something he knew he had never got quite right. 'A goat,' he continued, 'is always killed for a foreigner.'

'Are there many foreigners?' I questioned.

'A foreigner is any person – mostly Tubu – who's travelled a long way, but sometimes it can just mean a local who has been away from home for a while.'

Four men emerged out of the dark and quietly settled around us, so that we became a circle of murmuring conversation.

'One of the children asked,' Ahmet continued, 'if you would be able to stay for a few days.' It was nice to hear and, reclining against my pack, I looked up at a sky filled with glittering crumbs of light as the soothing purr of the Tubu swirled around me, like a docile eddy in some peaty pool of a woodland burn.

*   *   *

The following day, before dusk, we arrived at Bortou – another dune-top settlement – and were settled into a tent that quickly became filled with men eager to hear our news. The Tubu's generosity was inspiring. Time and again, with no warning of our arrival, everything we required was put at our disposal. A segment of the tent was peeled back, like the wing of a paper aeroplane, and I watched a goat's severed windpipe contract and expand in search of air, as a man remained quietly at the animal's side – his right palm gently on its flank – until the scuffling had stopped.

About an hour before we had reached Bortou, we came across two cameleers. One of them was returning to Sassai, so Omar brought him up to date with news of his village.

'What do the Tubu think of our journey across the Manga,' I asked after the cameleers had departed.

'They are astonished,' Ahmet replied, 'to see a white man who has the courage to do it.'

'*Courage*,' Omar interjected in his husky French.

'Also,' Ahmet persisted, 'that he rides his own camel and knows how to tie a turban well.'

These words, I knew, were not social pleasantries – they meant what they said. And, according to the Tubu, it was the first time in living memory a white person had travelled across the Manga.

As the tent became crowded with men of various ages, all I could see, from my perch at the back, was a throng of turbaned heads attentively listening to, or making polite enquiries of, my companions, as plumes of wispy heron-grey smoke curled and spun towards the roof, and hung there like an early morning mist. It felt as though our little cavalcade had become the Manga telegraph.

* * *

'There really is a feeling of moving into a different geographical and anthropological terrain,' I scribbled in my journal the following morning, 'and because of that we will, I presume, spend our nights – between Task and Birnin Kazoe – under the stars, rather than in the tent of some hospitable Tubu.' I had learnt from Ahmet that Task was the last Tubu village before

Birnin Kazoe. Until recently, and for as long as they could remember, the Tubu had sold their camels at Birnin Kazoe, and we would be travelling there along an ancient caravan path.

'Why don't the Tubu live below Task?' I asked, as the wind gusted outside. Ahmet translated the question to the five men in our tent.

'They say it's a different landscape,' Ahmet replied. 'That they don't want to live there – and nor do their animals.' Our visitors explained that while the Tubu and Arabs reared camels in the northern Manga, the Fulani bred cows in the south. As a rough guide, a line could be drawn between Nguigmi and Task: everything beneath it was home to the Fulani and the Kanuri, and to the north was Tubu. The Kanuri are a sedentary people who mostly live in the lands of the former Borno Empire (1380–93): north-east Nigeria, south-east Niger, western Chad and northern Cameroon.

'The Peul,' Ahmet explained, 'are particularly prevalent to the north-west of Diffa and to the south-east of Nguigmi.'

'Do you know how many Tubu live in the Manga?' I enquired.

'No one knows,' Ahmet answered after a short, reflective pause, and then offered me a glass of tea.

29

Bashir, our sinewy, patriarchal host, mounted his long-maned chestnut pony as our camels groaned and we lurched upwards on their backs. He had offered to guide us to Lyibilli, a Fulani encampment, where we would spend the night – between his village and Task; in short, we were being passed from one ethnic group to another, like pioneering explorers. It seemed Bashir had made a point of acquainting himself with his neighbours on the fringes of the Tubu's world and, as such, the Fulani's camp was an ethnic marker between the northern and southern Manga.

We found the Fulani a few hours later, after riding through an uncluttered landscape of rolling undulations. They were situated in a shallow basin seeded with bushy acacias, but it was like another country. These people looked different: 'Slender, fine featured, but dark skinned, with the profiles of Assyrian statues,' is how Rennell Rodd described the Fulani. Robes and turbans had vanished and the young men wore necklaces, earrings and bangles of colourful beads, and sported an array of flamboyant hats that appeared to have no uniformity of dress code at all; yet within the materials available to them, they were definitely aesthetes. They lived in an entirely different type of hut, both in structure and shape, and camels had been replaced with zebu. They had a different feeling about them: a more relaxed, even laissez-faire attitude, they spoke another language and they were not Muslims.

The small, igloo-shaped huts were made of thin, tightly packed branches and, from the back, resembled giant balls of garden twine that had been cut in half. Each couple or family appeared to have two of these huts: one for sleeping in and another for domesticity and, along with a delicate fence, pleated – from top to bottom – with narrow, pointed arches, the ensemble, with the sleeping quarters in the centre, was loosely shaped like a Cromer crab. It all felt very different from what I had become accustomed to, and when we dismounted from our camels I sensed a real distance between my companions and these people. Bashir, on the other hand, had forged a relationship with the encampment's patriarch: an affable stocky man, called Derri, who liked to laugh. The two of them, it appeared, had formed a friendship of mutual respect born from the sage understanding of families living on the tide line of different peoples.

Whenever Omar, Ahmet and I slept outside, our bedding was, as a matter of routine, laid in front of a bush – our heads pointed towards it, as if it were a wind shelter. The Fulani, however, had invited us to bed down on palm mats that had been carefully spread under a pleated barrier, but there was a slight slope, so if we did sleep with our heads beneath it – as if it were a bush – the blood would run to our heads. It became apparent that my companions recognised the dilemma and Ahmet, replacing habit with logic, suggested it might be more comfortable if we slept the other way round. After we rearranged ourselves, I huddled over my journal with the warmth of the fire caressing my shoulders and, looking up into the dusky middle distance, I became distracted by the inching progress of a silhouetted Tubu caravan, as it drifted along a ridge – a timeless image that seemed always to have belonged to the Sahel.

*   *   *

Shortly after dawn, Bashir headed back home and we trotted south towards Task – the Tubu's most southerly settlement. A few hours later, it appeared on a vast dune overlooking a savannah-like plain that had no ending in sight. If we had been in the Mediterranean, there might have been a Knights of St

John fortress – a stronghold against the Ottomans and the Barbary corsairs – perched on the hill's easterly promontory. One wonders how many woeful Caucasians did, by way of the Old Salt Road – from the North African littoral to the Sahel – end up as slaves in the sub-Saharan sultanates, long before Barth became the first recorded Christian to enter Agades in the mid-nineteenth century. And what of their extraordinary stories that died with them in enslaved obscurity? Yet maybe a voice has survived and, perhaps one day, a journal – unearthed at the bottom of a dusty trunk in Timbuktu's great library – will tell a European's tale of living in the Sahel during the seventeenth century.

30

'No white person has been here for a very long time,' Elhadji Mohamed Sale said, as his misty pupils peered into mine.

'How long?' I enquired, after listening to Ahmet's translation.

'A white woman came here,' he reflected, as if counting the decades in his mind, 'about forty years ago.'

'Would that have been Catherine Baroin?' I wondered. 'The anthropologist.'

'*Katerine*,' he chirped enthusiastically; his wrinkled face transforming into a collage of happy recognition. '*Katerine*.'

Elhadji Mohamed Sali, our Tubu host, was dressed in a white robe and turban and reclined along the side of a smoky tent. The pads of his right fingers lazily fiddled with a long necklace of Qur'anic prayer beads. His family's tents were situated in a valley on the other side of the steep dune that led up to Task.

'He wants to know,' Ahmet translated, 'if you would like to borrow a horse and investigate the valley.'

'Tell him – thanks,' I replied, 'but I'm going to rest for a while.' And I thought about how the valley might look in the rainy season: lush verdant meadows with huts, tents and family life, herds of goats and ponies grazing in fetlock-deep grass, and camels peering into the horizon, as if waiting for another season.

'Can I take a photograph of him?' I asked.

Ahmet translated and I watched him wince with surprise at the answer.

'He says,' Ahmet explained, looking confused, 'that you are *un blanc* and his decision not to let you take a photograph is because the whites abandoned them.'

Ahmet's expression changed from confusion to baffled frustration. He perched onto his knees – from his previously relaxed position on the rug – and explained to our host that the French had left because the people of Niger wanted their independence and, in addition, I was not French – but British.

'He says,' Ahmet continued, 'he thought all white people were French.'

'Can you tell him,' I answered deferentially, 'that I'm most certainly not French, and that Britain and France's history is littered with wars against each other.'

Ahmet translated and Elhadji Mohamed Sali listened, as if in studied contemplation, before giving an answer.

'He owns a lot of camels,' Ahmet translated. 'After the French left, he says there were many bandits who stole camels between Task and Termit but, when the French were here, bandits were shot. He says that these days, no one does anything about it. But,' Ahmet continued with an air of confusion, 'I don't think there are bandits here – as there's nowhere for them to hide.'

If there were bandits operating in the region I was relieved that, at least so far, we had avoided them. I became aware that our host's expression was changing, as if he had arrived at some important conclusion. He then uttered a few words and started to fumble with his wooden beads again.

'He says,' Ahmet said with a perplexed grin, 'because you are not French – you may take his photograph.'

I listened as Ahmet described how, after the French left the region, they dumped all their munitions into Lake Chad, and then he and Elhadji Mohamed Sali slipped into the beginnings of a long conversation, as if Ahmet was recounting our trip across the Manga, and our aged host was enquiring after old friends and acquaintances. At one point, Ahmet interjected:

'He remembers that very old sick man as *un grand* from when he was a small boy living in Termit.'

'Are you sure he was a hundred and twenty?' I asked again, as I was still pestered by doubt.

'I asked his sons,' Ahmet replied adamantly. 'The ones who were gathered outside his tent.'

'How old is Elhadji Mohamed?'

'Seventy-one,' Ahmet translated.

'And how old is *un grand*?'

'Someone who is in their forties or fifties,' Ahmet replied.

Elhadji then said something, as if asking a question.

'There has never,' Ahmet translated, 'been a British person here before, and he would like to know where Britain is.'

I smoothed out a large square in the sand on the floor of our tent and sketched an inaccurate map of Africa with my finger – highlighting Niger and the Manga, and their position in relation to Europe and Britain.

'Britain is north-west of here,' I said, pointing in the direction behind my shoulder. 'But,' I continued, bearing in mind the laconic wording of nomadic directions, 'it is much, much further than just "over that hill".'

'He has a bad back,' Ahmet said a while later. 'Do you have any more medicine left?'

I burrowed into the medical pack and handed over one of two remaining strips of paracetamol.

'If his back is that bad,' I suggested, 'he could always make the trip to the *Médicins Sans Frontières* clinic in Zinder. I know it's a long way, but in comparison to all the other Tubu villages we've stayed at, he is the closest to medical help.'

Ahmet repeated what I had said to Elhadji, who nodded and mumbled something.

'He thanks you for the information,' Ahmet replied, 'and said that Zinder is far, but he will think about it.'

My medical supplies were much depleted, but I had enjoyed being able to help where I could. There had been a startling lack of illness among the nomads, and the Tubu who had come to see me were mostly the elderly with back problems. There had been a couple of respiratory complaints, but disease – so overt on my travels from Niamey to Zinder – had seemingly evaporated. It appeared that nomadic living was not only good for the community, but healthy for the body and mind as well.

* * *

'*Tubu*,' Elhadji murmured the following afternoon, as I emerged from our tent coiling the last fold of my turban into place; his eyes narrowed in assessment, peering into my face, as the Qur'anic beads in his leathery, black fingers dangled in front of his robe. I do not know if he said it because of my appearance or because of our journey across the Manga. Nor can I remember if I smiled, but it was a warming affirmation as Omar, Ahmet and I climbed onto our camels in a squall of dust, then lurched upwards to a grumbling cacophony of growls and turned away from the Tubu's most southerly outpost. We were leaving the Tubu behind. I not only admired and envied their sense of community and geographical belonging, but I knew I would miss both them and their stark landscape.

We quickly found the ancient caravan path linking the Tubu to the markets in the south. As our camels trod through a terrain veiled in a quasi-coastal mist, we came across a ridge marked with the skeletons of two Fulani huts. They seemed to signal the beginning of a new land. The three of us settled into our riding positions – about fifteen metres apart from one another, with Omar in the centre – and walked through the gap between the abandoned constructions. Over the course of the next half hour, we passed two more deserted huts – one of which was surrounded by a rickety palisade, while the other had been taken over by a herd of zebu. Here, in the middle of the hut's remains, a white horned bull stood motionless, as if in occupancy. We had arrived in an entirely different terrain: a landscape marked by the increasing presence of trees, bushes, grass and a form of Sahelian broom called calimbo. The camels, their droppings, bones and carcasses, had all but disappeared and had been replaced by herds of zebu and their droppings, bones and carcasses.

The braided caravan path – honeycombed with mouse holes – threaded into the mist ahead of us and, as we swayed through a murky landscape, the light began to fade. We found a place to camp with a small clearing of sand bordered by three bushes; it was obviously a favoured Tubu stopover:

there were the telltale signs of ash-peppered mounds as well as lumps of charred wood, and, in addition, a neat row of kindling had been arranged, as though prepared by the last Tubu travellers in preparation for the next. It was the first sand clearing we had seen since leaving Task a few hours earlier, and my companions quickly took possession of the tiny island, as if the wispy, fawn-coloured grass encircling it was, from an accommodation point of view, a forbidden zone. Truly, the Tubu are a sand people. It is almost a given – at least for those living in the Manga – that they like to sit, sleep, cook, chat, eat and otherwise function in the stuff. Perhaps, that ring of sand was a representation of their identity – a manifestation of their patch of the Manga and, therefore, a space they could occupy entirely on their own terms.

31

I noticed, as we continued south the following morning, that the Fulani cameleers we saw in the middle distance did not turn towards us to say hello and, when we did manage to hail one of them in a quest for directions, there were none of the usual introductions and updates. It seemed that, as with many cultures, the Fulani and Tubu acknowledged each other's existence, but beyond that, there was a sense of estrangement and even masked suspicion between the two peoples. I had also observed, since Tororonga, that the Tubu cameleers we encountered – in contrast to the northern Manga – all carried cross-hilted swords carefully wedged horizontally alongside the camel's right flank.

'How long has Birnin Kazoe been there?' I enquired, as we rode past a herd of unattended goats.

'Since always,' Ahmet replied.

And, from my lofty perch, I watched the ancient caravan track – stamped into the ground by millions of hooves and feet over the centuries – spin away into the distance. I learnt from Ahmet that the Tubu did not travel this route as they had once done; in the last three years many had switched to the camel market in Boultoum, the frontier town situated sixty kilometres north of Birnin Kazoe and, as such, much closer to the Tubu.

'How many vets are there in the Manga?' I asked, thinking about the raw, oozing wound inflicted on my camel's flank by the constant rubbing of the wooden saddle.

'There are two: one in Nguigmi and the other is in Bouti.'

'And wells?'

'We need modern wells, but they cost CFA 10 million [£12,000] each,' Ahmet replied as he idly tapped a green, tendril-like branch against the side of his camel's neck. 'The wells made from wood don't last.'

'How many do you need?'

'Ten in the north; ten in the south; ten in the east and ten in the west,' Ahmet answered before translating his response to Omar who, after a moment's contemplation, nodded in agreement.

A wiry Fulani herder – carrying a staff crafted from a knobbly branch – appeared on the side of the trail; as we drew up alongside him, he gabbled a sentence.

'He salutes you,' Ahmet said with a grin.

'Please salute him back,' I answered. The herder beamed in response and, as he fell behind us, the caravan track began to splinter into different routes through a rolling valley of copses and bushes.

'This is a pretty valley,' I remarked.

'There are too many trees,' Ahmet replied.

For the next twenty-four hours we swayed through a mysterious and silent landscape laced with shawls of hovering mist, where cameleers momentarily appeared and then vanished. A small caravan of Fulani cameleers, on seeing we were trying to hail them, hastily retreated from us and soon disappeared.

'They probably thought, on seeing *un blanc*,' Ahmet snorted, 'we were Tuaregs and had brought the rebellion to the Manga.' His disdain of their suspicion and fear was palpable. 'Even the sand here is different,' he continued, glancing at the ground as if to suggest it was somehow inferior. 'Tubu sand,' he sniffed haughtily, 'is either orange or white.'

Then the land changed into a terrain of tor-like outcrops and, with their arrival, isolated mud abodes, enclosed by perimeter walls, appeared. This heralded the cultivating Kanuri. In the immediate vicinity of the tiny settlements was a scattering of small fields of stubble: mud huts and fields, sedentary domesticity and arable farming – we were fast moving out of the nomadic realm that had been our home for the last three weeks, yet there was still no sign or feeling of the modern world. We could have been travelling in the early nineteenth century, as we followed the trail past hamlets abandoned as if in hibernation and built only for seasonal use.

32

The caravan path curled around the bend of a cliff and Laraba came into view. Unmarked on my map and situated in the neck of a vast valley, it was, by Sahelian standards, a small town. At the foot of a mountainous ridge, it looked as if it had been lost in time and, from a distance, appeared fortified. There was a sprinkling of bushy foliage among the sepia walls and a sporadic, but constant, muffled pounding arose from the settlement, like the dull popping of old champagne corks. Laraba, at first sight, resembled a miniature version of Agades. Outside the town, were the snaking tracks of two dried-up riverbeds. 'Wow,' I murmured unintentionally, while I absorbed what was unfolding in front of me. My camel's ears pricked forward as hydraulic-seeming hooves cautiously negotiated the scree-littered trail and, alongside our companions, we slowly descended to the valley floor and rode towards Laraba.

The peculiar popping sound grew louder as we approached the outskirts; at times, there seemed to be a cascading rhythm to the noise and, high up on our camels, we could see – over mud walls – colourfully clad women pounding millet with giant wooden pestles, their bodies heaving gracefully over large wooden mortar-like bowls. Each enclosed or semi-enclosed compound harboured a thatched, conical abode and what looked like storerooms were built into the surrounding interior walls. We stopped at the end of a sandy alley and, as our camels sank to the ground, an old man in a purple robe wearing a colourfully embroidered Hausa-style hat walked over to us.

'Has a white man ever been here before?' I asked.

The old man said something.

'Never,' Ahmet translated.

'A white man on a camel!' the elderly man exclaimed in pidgin French, his sheeny eyes wide with disbelief.

'When was this place founded?' I continued.

'He says,' Ahmet explained after listening to the old man's response, 'that he doesn't even know his own age, let alone how old Laraba is – but he knows it was built in the time of his great-grandfather.'

Just like Henry Barth, on his arrival in Agades and Zinder a century and a half earlier, we were quickly given somewhere to stay, and our camels were hobbled and led out to graze. The self-contained building we were offered – a narrow room about six metres long – was hastily prepared with three mattresses; the lodging itself was situated inside a private enclosure that, in part, was encircled by a barricade. 'I truly think Barth must have felt as I do now after arriving in Agades or Zinder with his local guides,' I scribbled in my journal an hour later. 'I would never have been able to do this journey without my Tubu companions, who, despite the different ethnic cultures that exist in the Manga, have an intricate understanding of Manga protocol.'

* * *

Salih, another wizened man, attired in a robe and patterned lemon, lime and red hat, volunteered to introduce us to his chief. Ahmet and I followed him along a warren of sandy alleys until we arrived at the entrance of a walled enclosure, where we found the headman sitting cross-legged on a rug under a canopy which gave the appearance of an audience chamber. Behind us, while Salih introduced us to the hereditary chief, a small group of young men stood as if they were sons at court seeking paternal favours. We sat down opposite the potentate and Ahmet began to converse with him in Kanuri.

'He confirms,' Ahmet translated, 'that Laraba was founded in the time of his great-grandfather, which he thinks was about a hundred and seventy years ago.'

That means, I thought, it was founded in 1840 – just a decade before Barth arrived in Agades.

'Has a white man been here before?' I said, looking for clarification.

'He says a white person came to visit the ancient site on the mountain above here about sixteen years ago, but he did not enter Laraba,' Ahmet answered. 'Apart from that, he has never seen or heard of a white man coming here.' It rather seemed that tracts of the Manga, despite French colonisation, had been simply forgotten and overlooked – even when it was under the French government's administration.

'What ancient site is that?' I questioned.

'He says it was there before Laraba was built,' Ahmet replied. 'No one knows who built it or how old it is. He asks if you would like to see it?'

'Definitely,' I replied. 'Could you also ask him if there is any rock art in the surrounding mountains?'

'He says there is not, but some of his people will take us to the ancient site.'

The shrivelled chief looked beleaguered by age and whittled away by life; there was no sparkle left in his clouded eyes and, in his stare, he seemed to be observing me through the lens of an inverted telescope. I was not even sure if he could see me as a clear, visible image.

We left the chief to his solitary ruminations and, accompanied by six craggy Kanuri elders, walked across the network of winding lanes, before beginning to scramble up the rocky slopes under an intensely glaring midday sun. Along the crest of the ridge overlooking the plain-like valley, we found a periphery wall – constructed from boulders – that encircled a position about the size of eight tennis courts. At a glance, it looked as if it might have once harboured a fortified settlement, but judging from the absence of dwelling foundations, it might have been built simply as a retreat in times of hostilities. Some of the boulders in the wall were so large it would have taken several men to move and position them into place, and I began to wonder who were the people who built it, when and why?

Beneath us, Laraba looked splendidly romantic, nestling in its wilderness setting. As I gazed over the two dried-up river beds – which I later discovered were called *Loulouno* and *Wadjadja* – it was not hard to imagine the view in the aftermath of the rains, when the rivers became alive: children playing, splashing, giggling and swimming in the meandering currents of cool, gushing water, when the surrounding desert was transformed into a green prairie. For as long as anyone could remember the Tubu had camped outside Laraba on their way to Birnin Kazoe, but, as they had mostly ceased to use the market there, it was primarily the Fulani who now travelled along the caravan trail – a route forgotten in time and completely bypassed by the Western world.

We clambered back down the rock face and, immediately outside Laraba, there was a group of vibrantly dressed girls whose heads, like their mothers', were wrapped in a vivid array of scarves. They sat in the dappled shade scraping knife blades over long green stems and, from the allotted piles beside each of them, it was apparent they were performing a community chore, rather than any recreational activity. As we progressed into the village and through the alleys, a crowd of children and adults followed us towards our lodgings – at times we could barely proceed as they enthusiastically pressed against us.

'Can you ask,' I said to Ahmet, 'the elder next to you if he knows how many people live here?'

Ahmet translated my enquiry. 'About a thousand – he thinks.'

Even Ahmet and Omar, in their reserved Tubu way, were visibly impressed by our reception and minor-celebrity status, and I saw them smile in a way they had not done before. The privacy of our lodgings was a welcome relief, but the crowd did not disperse and they waited on the other side of the palisade in an effort to steal a glimpse of a white person. There was the odd evidence of the twentieth century I had noticed as we strolled across Laraba: large metal bowls like those I had seen for sale in Zinder's market, the occasional piece of nylon clothing and a few tatty fragments of black plastic, but that was all. It was as if the people of Laraba had found the fringes of the modern world, but the modern world had yet to find them.

A peculiarity I discovered afterwards, when poring over photographs of the Larabians, was a shot of an adolescent girl wearing a necklace of silver coins, identical to the Hapsburg one I had bought at the market in Nguigimi – perhaps just another example of the age-old drifting movement of goods from the Mediterranean to the Sahel and vice versa.

33

We left Laraba after a stay of only a few hours and continued along the trail and across the plain. Within sight of Laraba were a couple of villages, on the crest of rippling undulations: one of them was called 'Little Laraba'. They were the first of a handful of villages we encountered in the ensuing twenty-four hours, and they each looked as if they had been founded specifically to service the traffic between the Manga and Birnin Kazoe. The Kanuri's fields fell away, and the Fulani's nomadic encampments reappeared among tangled copses. The grass, in the immediate vicinity of the caravan route, had been decimated by herds of zebu and goats in transit, and with each passing kilometre that took us closer to the market – and back to the frontiers of civilisation – it became harder to find fodder for our camels, which were beginning to manifest the effects of our rigorous journey.

*   *   *

'Omar says,' Ahmet explained in the shadows of a magma-coloured sunset, 'that Laraba is the end of the Manga and the beginning of the Damergou.' Our journey was drawing to an end, yet, within the daily routine, we had become familiar with each other's presence, habits and silent moods. As they prayed beside me on the camel rugs, with embers spitting and hissing behind them, it was as if we had known each other for an age and, like old companions, were comfortable with the rela-tionships we had created. However, we were tired and only a couple of days earlier Ahmet and I had slipped into a fractious conversation about the first Tuareg rebellion.

'Ahmet,' I asked him, 'there's something I don't understand. I thought the peace agreement between the Tuaregs and the government was signed in 1995, but you left the Tuareg rebels after a peace treaty in 1992.'

'Yes,' he replied. 'There was a treaty in 1992.'

Omar uttered what appeared to be a question, and I asked Ahmet to translate.

'He said he thought there was only one peace treaty.' A shiver of frustration passed across Ahmet's face and it seemed our questioning of the rebellion's chronology was irritating him.

'So, when was the Tubu massacre?' I asked.

'They were taken from the town of Bosso, and killed in Boulatoungour.'

'Can you remember when that was?' I persisted, as I wanted to understand if the killings were the trigger point of the Tubu rebellion or if it was an event that happened after the Tubu had allied themselves with the Tuareg rebels.

'Myself and the only other Tubu politician went to see the president after those murders,' he answered. 'I told the president: "It was inhuman".'

'Yes, so you said... but the year of the massacre...'

'Sometimes your French,' he snapped, 'can be incomprehensible.'

'So... can yours!' I growled, after assessing the risk of my answer to the former rebel. I had become increasingly frustrated by Ahmet's sometimes-dismissive attitude to my enquiries. Journal data is crucial – like collating the pieces of a one-off jigsaw puzzle. We both sat there for a moment staring at each other in defiant silence.

Omar, as though pondering on some fact after revisiting his life as a rebel, then said something: it seemed to be a question about a chronological detail. Ahmet – his focus distracted – swivelled on his haunches and, like a predatory snake about to lunge at a carefree frog, verbally launched into Omar. However, his irritation was quickly diffused by Omar's imperturbability and the conversation trailed off into a silence that was devoid of any brooding. It was the only time on our journey that there was a cross sentence. And, in conclusion, I later discovered that there were two treaties between the Tuaregs and the Niger government: 'The National Pact' signed in Mali on 11 April 1992 at Bamako, and 'The Peace Agreement' which was negotiated three years later in Ouagadougou on 15 April 1995.

As for the massacre, nine hundred and fifty Tubu – who fled to Nigeria in the wake of the rebellion – were captured in October 1998, just two months after the signing of the peace agreement between the Tubu rebel group *Front Démocratique Révolutionnaire* (FDR) and the Niger government in N'Djamena. Rounded up in a joint military operation involving Chad, Niger and Nigeria, the Tubu were handed over to Nigérien troops, and the women and children were separated from their husbands. The men were never seen again, though in January 1999 a mass grave was discovered on the island of Boulatoungour on Lake Chad in the Diffa region. The Niger government denied there had been any killings but, three months later, the High Commissioner for the Restoration of Peace confirmed the existence of the grave and, in it, the remains of a hundred and fifty men – whose names were subsequently published in the press. Ahmet had explained, when we were in the northern Manga, that as a Tubu politician he had been taken to the mass grave. As he referred to the gruesome horrors of what he had been shown, his expression displayed a sort of morose desolation.

*   *   *

The following morning a Fulani horseman joined us and, like drifting on a placid current, we swayed south towards the shores of civilisation.

'When was this village built?' Ahmet asked a middle-aged Kanuri, as we rode through another nineteenth-century-looking settlement.

'How can I answer that?' the Kanuri replied, in the same vein as the Larabians. 'I don't even know how old I am... but it was established in the time of my grandfather.'

The village was called Gadmour. If we had been in the Taklamakan and stumbled across the ruins of such a place, it would have been a formidable Old Silk Road discovery. Yet here we were travelling down an active and ancient caravan route – complete with living villages and cultures that predated colonial Africa.

Shortly after Gadmour we arrived at a ridge overlooking another vast plain, where the trail descended through a narrow gorge to the valley floor. It was as if we were travelling through a portal; the doorway to the Manga was closing behind us and, with it, access to the hidden world of those who lived there. As we approached a nest of wells among a sprawling grove of acacias, I glanced over my shoulder and, in doing so, felt a bubble of sadness – as though we had merged with the main artery of a jungle river that would soon arrive at the river delta. A kind of time-traveller who had been shown a way of life and community that, in many ways, the modern world had mislaid, I now had to return to the realm from where I had come. There was even a different feeling at the wells, as if the Fulani watering their herds were somehow affected by twenty-first century vibrations.

Towering mountain outcrops rose out of the valley floor, and their flat, field-like summits might have been designed as UFO landing pads. In the middle ground ahead of us, a horse, with rider in saddle, rose up on its hind legs – front legs paddling the air – and then galloped off in a cloud of dust.

'My fleece,' I exclaimed, feeling around for it behind my saddle cushion. 'It's gone.'

'It doesn't matter,' Ahmet said. 'It is only an item of clothing.'

'You don't understand,' I continued. 'It contains my passport and permissions. We need them for when we arrive at Birnin Kazoe.' Two Tubu heading south from the direction of the Tuareg rebellion, with a white man bereft of any identification or permissions, would not look good for any of us. I quickly revisited the last moment I remembered seeing my fleece: the wells at the foot of the gorge. 'We must go back the way we came,' I said.

Ahmet explained the dilemma to Omar, who, with his usual calm demeanour, turned his camel around and, studying the ground, exactly retraced our camels' footsteps. 'Someone might steal it,' I mumbled with growing anxiety.

'Not around here they won't,' Ahmet replied – and he meant it.

Twenty minutes later we met three Fulani riders trotting towards us from the direction of the wells. Not only had they found my fleece, but they also wanted to reassure us that the passport and permissions were still safely in one of the pockets. It was yet another testament to the nomads' honesty and transparency.

'I knew we would find it,' Ahmet chortled. 'My spirit was still.'

I felt the moisture being sucked from the pores of my skin as I curled a fold of turban over my nose. Giant, spiralling dust devils twisted, squall-like, across the barren valley floor ahead of us. As we rode side by side, all traces of the Manga had disappeared. Small villages, dotted along the lower ridges of mountainous undulations, appeared in the distance and we passed a market, where two Kanuri women approached us wanting to know, as we were Tubu travelling south, if we had any dates for sale. As we progressed, I became aware of rows of ancient man- made mounds, like abandoned anthills, that were intermittently spaced across the valley floor, every fifty metres or so. It was as if we were travelling past an age-old grid belonging to some vanished and forgotten civilisation; perhaps even built by the same enigmatic people who constructed the site above Laraba.

34

It began as a vague, blurry wisp and then the suggestion became a neat plume of dust, as a motorbike bolted across our path, far in the distance. Like a salmon about to snatch a passing fly I felt, within that plume, that I was being hooked back into the twenty-first century. The Manga already seemed to belong to another time – and another world. And then, as if on cue, Omar was tapping on his mobile to see if there was any reception. There had been no network since Nguigmi, but now, before I knew what was happening, he thrust the phone into my hands. '*Ministre*,' he said urgently. '*Ministre*.' I had no idea to whom he was referring, as I listened to the distorted voice at the other end. I thought perhaps it might be someone from the Ministry of Tourism, and that Omar had called to say we were safely across the Manga and would soon be arriving at Birnin Kazoe.

'*Bonjour*,' I said. '*Ça va?*'

'*Ça va bien*,' the voice replied. '*Merci*.'

'I've had a fantastic trip across the Manga,' I said enthusiastically. 'Omar and Ahmet have been brilliant.'

'Perhaps,' the voice continued, 'we could meet at the Ministry when you get back into Niamey. How about Monday?'

'If I've got time,' I answered. There was a pause on the other end of the line, at which point I realised it was Issa Lamine, Minister of Health and former rebel leader of the FDR. 'Definitely,' I speedily recovered. 'I'll be there.'

'Good,' he replied.

'The Manga is very beautiful,' I continued, rather clumsily.

'*Oui*,' he answered, with a polite chuckle that was tinged with surprise.

'*Alors, à Lundi*,' I said, keen to wrap up the slightly surreal conversation I was having on the back of a camel with one of Niger's most important men.

'Monday,' he confirmed. 'At the Ministry.'

'He wants to see me when I get back to Niamey,' I explained, leaning over and returning the phone to Omar.

'You *must* wear your Tubu robes and turban when you meet him,' Ahmet suggested, and Omar earnestly nodded in agreement.

I had returned to the twenty-first century. As Ahmet explained how Omar was in some way related to Issa Lamine, we approached a road – the first I had seen in a month. It looked as if someone had placed a ruler across the landscape and penned a thick line through it, as though it was the boundary of a country that had been demarcated at the 1885 Berlin Conference. It was totally out of keeping with the world to which I had become accustomed since leaving Nguigmi and, as our camels stepped over it, I felt a peculiar sensation, as if we should not be travelling by camel any more – even though there was no traffic. And then, in front of us, as we slipped onto a sandy track that meandered away from the road, lay a seemingly untrammelled panorama that felt, and looked like, the beginnings of an entirely different land.

*　　*　　*

We camped on an escarpment along with other nomads en route to the market. About a dozen fires flickered around us – all Fulani – and there was a feeling that we were the advance guard of an invasion force. It was noteworthy how, being only five kilometres from Birnin Kazoe, the nomads kept a particularly vigilant eye on their herds. They freely admitted to their suspicions of towns – and the people who lived in them. A wizened Fulani brought some wood over to us – an increasingly scarce asset the closer we approached Birnin Kazoe – and another scraggy, middle-aged man, Kirri, settled on his haunches around our fire. He had travelled from a village called Diguini, near Tasker, and was hoping to sell a few rams. He made the trip, down the same caravan path we had followed, five times a year and he confirmed that the larger of the two rivers outside Laraba was called *Loulouno*. Kirri sometimes dug wells, a trade he had learnt from his father, and charged CFA 7,000 for every two metres of depth.

'He says,' Ahmet translated, 'that he's dug about thirteen wells – but they probably don't last long and need "topping up" every couple of years.' Kirri then gabbled something, as though asking a question, and Ahmet replied. 'He wanted to know where we had come from,' Ahmet explained, with an air of concealed amusement. 'He said he had heard of Nguigmi, but had never been there and didn't really know where it was.'

*   *   *

The saddle-wound on my camel, I discovered as our surroundings became draped in the gloaming blue shades of dawn, was raw almost to the bone, and had started to ooze a gooey, transparent liquid. Only the day before he had almost tried to bite me as I mounted: his bearded head twisting around with the dexterity of an irritated snake – as if poised for imminent attack – and I found myself peering into the animal's gurgling throat with a certain helpless anticipation of a lunge that, fortunately, never came.

Our last camp fell away, as papery leaves tumbled and skipped across the ground, and dust billowed around us. Like driftwood, collecting on the approach to a wild river's mouth, we found ourselves in the market's current. Either ahead or to the side of us, the Fulani herded camels, goats, donkeys and zebu towards the town. We had left the last of the wilderness behind the previous day; the landscape around us was flat, mundane, drab and covered in a gritty membrane of dust. By the time we reached a sign that read 'BIRNIN KAZOE', the wind had subsided, the skies had cleared and the sun burned above us. It was odd to see a conurbation again. The near-immediate collision and juxtaposition of the centuries and cultures – from yesterday's lost world in the Manga to Birnin Kazoe's trucks and machine guns – seemed to have the effect of heightening my senses.

Omar suggested we dismount prior to reaching the police barrier, so we walked the last hundred metres of our journey. A jeep with four armed men, one of whom stood in the back propped against the cabin roof with an AK47, sped past us heading north towards the Tuareg rebellion. As we arrived at the military control post, the authorities could not have been more convivial and helpful.

'Where have you come from?' a soldier asked curiously, while Omar briefed the police about our travels.

'From Nguigmi to Termit and, from there, through Torronga and Task – to here,' I answered.

The soldier gave a protracted whistle that slowly tailed off into a breathy exhalation, as if highlighting the distance we had covered.

Omar beckoned me into a small room, where I removed my permit and passport and handed them to a lean policeman. 'We had been advised there was a white man in the area,' the policeman said in French, and he stamped a circular, mauve imprint at the bottom of my authorisation. I was pleased the authorities in Zinder had notified them.

'Do you want to take a photograph of your arrival here to mark the end of your journey?' the whistling soldier enquired.

'No,' I replied. 'I think I'll leave it.' But, in hindsight, I rather wish we had.

Some Tubu appeared who, yet again, appeared to be friends of Omar and, walking a short distance through the town with the camels in tow, we stopped outside a door. '*Sho, sho, sho,*' I urged, and my camel lurched backwards and forwards before collapsing onto its knees. We unloaded our kit and lugged it into the small courtyard behind the street door, and then, amongst the swirl of introductory activity, I became aware that our camels were being led away to find fodder. I did not know, as I watched them stream down the bustling lane out of sight, that it was the last time I would see them.

We were shown into a room with a few mattresses; in the corner, a Tubu was brewing some tea on a bed of orange charcoal as if we were back in the desert. Ten other Tubu soon joined us and they all wanted to know about our journey and of news from across the Manga. It felt as though we were sitting in one of the beetle-like tents again, as I was offered a small glass of tea.

'They are astonished and amazed at our journey,' Ahmet volunteered. 'It's not just the distance we did, but the speed at which we covered it that they're impressed with.' He looked happy, relaxed – even serene. I think all three of us felt the same way. 'Our host says that you have become a Tubu,' Ahmet translated.

As I lay there reclining on my side, facing the other men and with my body propped up on my elbow, I asked Ahmet if it was possible to wash. I was led across the courtyard to a doorway that opened into a roofless stone cubicle. I thanked my host, twisted the tap and, before removing my robes, gazed at the water, as it curled into a whirlpool around the drain in the centre of the concrete floor. It was the first time I had seen my body in three weeks, and I found it freckled with colonies of pink and red pustules: my legs, the tops of my feet and my knees were all dotted with a patterning of grubby, inflamed abrasions. I scrubbed the mass of tangled and clumped follicles on my head, and watched the foaming shampoo slop onto the floor and disappear down the drain in a creamy stream. I crouched down, leant my head under the tap and rinsed my hair until it started to squeak. My hands then darted over my body with an oval bar of soap, and the slimy liquid splashed to the ground. As I rubbed myself dry and got dressed in a pair of khaki trousers and a T-shirt, the sounds of a frontier town cluttered with activity swirled around and over the cubicle.

Returning to our room, still inundated with Tubu, I handed over my robe and turban to Omar as he had organised someone to wash our clothes. Although I did not know it then, I had worn them for the last time. They did not return until the evening, by which time a seat had been reserved for me early the following morning in the cabin of a dilapidated truck that was going to Zinder.

'Why are the Tubu here so impressed with our journey?' I asked Ahmet, with genuine puzzlement.

'Because you are brave,' Ahmet replied. 'And these town Tubu cannot do such a journey as we have just done.' It was humbling to hear and, as I penned in my journal later that afternoon in a room filled with robed and turbaned Tubu, I felt extraordinarily at peace and at one with myself.

I did not want any millet, as I watched the men huddle around the communal bowl, and an adolescent boy led me from our quarters and out into the distorted cacophony of the street. I squinted in the glare, as we strolled past a man in a bedraggled suit who was crouching in the hollow of a rubbish dump beside a small fire, as if it was his home. The market was situated almost opposite to where we were lodged, and I followed my guide through a maze of stalls bustling with early-afternoon activity; weaving past the Tubu with their cross-hilted swords and arm daggers; the Fulani with their bows, quivers and short swords, and the Kanuri who seemed to prefer an appearance free of any weaponry.

I was shown into a small shack in the market's hub, which offered a dark stew of intestines and couscous, and a ladle of each was dunked onto a plate for me. I noticed that in the stall opposite there was a neat pile of honeycomb-coloured bread, so, briefly leaving my plate, I sauntered over and bought a loaf and a couple of bottles of Coca Cola. The bread itself was exquisitely soft when I dunked a piece into the russet-coloured sauce that was seasoned with spices I remembered from the market in Agades. This plate of food – a dish I simply would not have touched a month ago - was delicious and, enhanced by the cool sips of fizzy drink, it was the most savoury and stimulating meal I had eaten in weeks.

After I had finished, I bought half a dozen bottled drinks for myself, Omar and Ahmet and, as I was doing so, a small crowd of children gathered around me and stared. 'They're not being rude,' an amiable man observed in fluent French. 'It's just that they've never seen a white person before.'

'Truly,' I replied. 'I really don't mind.' Everything felt so natural – as if I had somehow become a part of it all – and it would have been difficult to be irritated by anything. I found my own way back to our lodgings and, on my return, flipped open two bottles of Coca-Cola with the Leatherman, and handed one each to Omar and Ahmet who, as they slowly drank them, looked like boys with hard-earned lollipops.

As the afternoon progressed, Omar suggested he would like to buy my camels instead of another buyer he had found for them. I was pleased with this arrangement. They could not have found a more caring owner and I knew that the sore on my camel's back would quickly heal. I had been silently concerned as to their fate, with whom they might end up and what might happen to them. I gave Omar the saddles and everything else that was left over from our provisions, and he bundled up a plastic bag of dried dates for me.

'This is for you,' I said to Omar, after removing my medical bag, 'because you are always in the desert and bush. And this,' I continued, handing a suede book of blank sheets I had bought in London, 'is for you Ahmet. Perhaps you can use it for a journal,' I suggested. 'How about – Memoirs of a Manga Tubu?'

The muezzin's mellifluous call soared through the late afternoon: 'Allāhu Akbar... Allāhu Akbar,' the voice chanted. 'Allāhu Akbar... Allāhu Akbar,' the summons continued, as each note delicately floated through the air with the lightness of falling breast-feathers. As the sweet-sounding chords of Islam hovered around us, Omar, Ahmet and the other Tubu filed out of the room to pray at the mosque, and I was left alone to scribble in my journal. A while later I stepped into the courtyard and, thinking I was alone, began to slowly pace across its breadth in contemplation. As I walked past the tiny alley that led out onto the street, I was surprised to find Omar and Ahmet concealed in the shadows of the fading light. They had obviously just returned from the mosque.

'What are you two doing hiding there?' I was about to ask jocularly, when I noticed that Ahmet's eyes had welled up.

'Our souls have touched,' he said looking into my eyes.

I slowly nodded in recognition. It was an extraordinary moment, as though we had arrived on a plane where anything was possible between humans. Maybe, in part, the sensation was seeded in our shared wilderness routine, as if like three streams merging into a single flow, we had travelled as a tributary of combined energy across the Manga and our separation would feel peculiar for a while, until our energies were reconfigured by the necessity of adjustment. Omar settled his hand on Ahmet's shoulder, as if they were brothers, and steered him towards the doorway onto the street.

'To the market,' Omar gently suggested, and they slipped out of sight.

I sat on a rickety chair in the courtyard tinted by dusk's cerulean shades. Everything around me then became surrounded by a luminous glow, as if in a Qi Gong state of being, which was perhaps born out of the amalgam of our recent travelling regime.

*   *   *

'Is it really safe for me to travel to Zinder through this part of the country?' I later asked Ahmet in a room filled with tea-drinking Tubu.

'If anyone touches you,' he snarled, as his pupils narrowed into those bayonets of his, 'they'll have a fight with the Tubu.' Our relationship had arrived at such a level of understanding that his statement did not require any acknowledgment from me. 'It will be odd,' Ahmet ruminated, 'when you have gone.'

'Only for a few days,' I replied.

'A few days,' he pondered. 'A few days.'

*   *   *

The following morning, before dawn, I awoke to the azan and a flurry of rustling, as Omar and Ahmet coiled their turbans into place. The muezzin's summons floated through the darkness:

Allāhu Akbar (God is most great)
Ashhadu anna la ilāha illa Allāh (I bear witness there is no God but God)
Ashhadu anna Muḥammadan rasūl Allāh (I bear witness Muhammad is the prophet of God)
Hayya ʿalā al-ṣalāt (Come to prayer)
Hayya ʿalā al-falāḥ (Come to well-being)
Al-ṣalāt khayrun min al-nawm (Prayer is better than sleep)
Allāhu Akbar (God is most great)
Lā ilāha illa Allāh (There is no God but God)

As the room emptied of Tubu, Omar and Ahmet disappeared out into the night. I had spent a month sleeping on the ground, and had become accustomed to it. After shaving, something I had continued to do every day as I found it refreshing, I made a final check of my pack and knapsack and bundled up my rug.

And then it all happened so quickly: Omar and Ahmet returned from their prayers, accompanied me outside to a truck laden with sacks, bags and passengers, and my pack was tied into place in a safe anchorage that someone recruited as a seat, then I was shown into a cold, draughty cabin that was caged in shattered glass and peeling rubber.

'I prefer riding a camel,' I said to Ahmet, as I slipped into the cramped seat.

'Be careful with him,' Ahmet replied, as if in counsel to the driver. 'He knows how to ride a camel.'

As the silence was shattered by the raucous sound of an awakening diesel engine, I leant out of the window and looked back firstly at Omar, then Ahmet – a last frame of each of them so I would not forget, and then the lorry lumbered down the dilapidated street and out into a landscape obscured by dust, as if we were travelling through a winter fog.

35

I arrived back at *Les Roniers* two days later. I already missed Omar, Ahmet, their habits and how they prayed beside me, and I missed the Tubu way of life: their robes, turbans, quiet conversation and their straw-coloured Chinese tea. I missed the camels – each of them as individuals – particularly the way Ahmet's used to hum before, during and immediately after being loaded up, and I missed the rhythm and sensation of being on a camel. The only thing I did not miss was the smell of a camel's breath. After the five-hour lorry journey across sandy tracks to Zinder, I received a call from Ahmet on my mobile to see if I had arrived safely.

'We are,' he explained, 'at the place we camped with the Fulani two nights ago.' He went on to describe how my white camel was in tow and unencumbered by baggage. I was pleased at this news as it meant his saddle wound would soon heal. As I listened, Ahmet's voice began to fragment and then, seconds later, the fractured dialogue was replaced by satellite silence. It was the last time I heard their voices – heading north with our camels towards the Manga.

*   *   *

'We thought and worried about you,' Annie said, enfolding me in a hug, as I stepped into *Les Roniers'* Provençal restaurant. 'I was talking to some Tuareg friends about what you were doing with the Tubu, and even they said you had to be extremely careful.'

'There was no need to worry,' I reassured her. 'But thanks.' It was a tender welcome. I was invited to dine with her and Pierre at their corner table overlooking the ground-floor restaurant and, as I told them about the Manga, I savoured each mouthful of my brochette, green beans and chips.

*   *   *

The following morning I asked Harouma, the taxi man, if he could drive me to the Health Ministry. We parked outside a tall municipal building that was on a protected island of its own. I walked into the lobby and explained to the armed guard that I had spoken with the minister on the phone and had come to make an appointment with his secretary. He smiled, provided some laconic directions, and pointed towards the stairs as a couple of robed Tubu glided past. I climbed the steps and found the secretary's office – opposite Issa Lamine's – where a smartly dressed Tubu sat behind a mahogany-coloured desk that was piled with paperwork. There were three other men in the room who were casually sitting on a long sofa, and I knew at a glance they were Tubu.

'I've just crossed the Manga by camel with the Tubu,' I explained. 'I spoke to the minister four days ago and have come here to arrange a meeting on Monday.'

'Your journey with the Tubu,' he replied, 'is very good.' It was as if he had already been briefed. 'The minister isn't here on Monday, but perhaps you could see him now?'

I had not expected this. I was dressed in khaki trousers and a T-shirt.

'Good,' I answered.

I followed the secretary across the corridor and into a pristine waiting room where several official-looking people were collected. The secretary knocked on a door, which obviously led into the minister's office, and slowly proceeded to open it, before saying something as if in explanation. He closed the door and, a few moments later, a man emerged from the office and I was guided in. It was a comfortable, spacious ministerial room, almost palatial in comparison to the other offices I had visited in Niamey. Everything was clean and tidy, and the carpet had a soft tread. There was a long desk at the end of the room, decorated with a small flag of Niger, where a few objects and papers were carefully arranged. Behind a plush black leather chair were some elegant cabinets, and above them hung the official framed portrait of President Mamadou Tandja.

To the right, as I walked in, was a low glass table that was encircled by sofa-chairs; on top of it were arranged a large bowl of fruit, a pen, a mobile and some sheets of paper. Issa Lamine, Minister of Health and former rebel leader of the *Front Démocratique Révolutionnaire*, sat in a sofa positioned against the wall. He had a large frame, and his camouflage-green robes – made from a matted material unlike anything I had seen the Tubu wear – billowed around and over his twin-seated sofa. He had a certain presence, and looked like a person used to holding audiences, be it in Niamey or in the desert. And he radiated the same air of imperturbability as Omar did. Indeed, with his roundish face, rather than the long wiry Arabic features possessed by some Tubu, he looked as though he was related to my Manga guide.

'*Wossara?*' he said.

'*Wossou.*' I replied.

'We all think,' the minister continued in French, while beckoning me to sit down, 'that what you have done is a good thing.'

'I understand no white person has been into the Manga for at least half a century or more.'

'This is true,' he replied. 'The French did a bad thing when they wrote about the Tubu. They said the Tubu were dangerous and killed men. This is simply not true.'

The minister's mobile started to vibrate and, looking at the number illuminated on the screen, he took the call.

After he had finished his short conversation, I spoke again: 'Omar and Ahmet told me that about forty wells are needed in the Manga.'

'Forty is a lot,' Lamine replied. 'Twenty good wells at CFA ten million each would probably do it. The Tubu need wells – and wells that last. Water is everything. If there's no water the animals start to die and then the people start to die. With desertification they can't find the right wood to build the wells properly and those that are built traditionally only last for months – not years. These new wells last for years.'

'What about doctors?' I enquired. 'I noticed it was really only the elderly who appeared to suffer. The other generations seemed to manage very well. I gave all my medicine to them,' I said as an afterthought.

'Well done,' he answered. 'There are a few cases of TB, but otherwise it's pretty good. We do what we can medically.'

I explained that I had told Omar I would leave my blanket for him to collect when he was next in Niamey. 'Could I leave it with your secretary?' I asked, as I knew Omar would be in touch with Issa Lamine at some point.

'Yes,' he replied. 'Here is my card. Call me when you are next in Niamey.'

I thanked him, and returned to the secretary's office to explain about the rug that I would drop off with him. The other Tubu were still casually sitting on the sofa, and I heard one of them say that our trip across the Manga was *extraordinaire*. It was good to be among the Tubu again.

I walked down the stairs, across the lobby and out into the glaring heat, where I found Harouma parked up against a barrier.

'Issa Lamine,' he said, twisting the key in the ignition, 'is the most respected politician in Niger. People trust him.'

We drove across Niamey to *Le Grand Hotel* and, as the warm air washed over my face and right arm, the Manga already felt like a long time ago – yet it had only been three days since I had left Omar and Ahmet in Birnin Kazoe. I ambled through the glass doors into the hotel and stepped into the booth-like bar. At one of the small round tables, I noticed Akly, who was in quiet conversation with a man and a woman.

'Any tourists?' I asked.

'There are none,' he muttered. 'Céline has taken a couple to Gao in Mali, but that is all.'

I strolled out onto the hotel's impressive terrace overlooking the glistening waters of the Niger, and squinted as I watched serpentine currents vanish into a mirror of sunlight. A sandwich and bottle of cola arrived on a tray, and I sat lost in thought at a table in the shade of a potted palm, listening to the muted sounds of a West African city beneath me. I then returned to the bar to say farewell to Akly and, as I was talking to him, I became aware that a women with him seemed familiar – and she seemed to remember me.

'I told you,' she exclaimed to Akly, 'I recognised him.'

It took me a few moments to place her. 'Katia,' I said. Her name slipped from my lips, as if her voice had unlocked a hidden repository in my memory.

'And,' she remarked, 'he remembers my name!'

Katia was Lebanese and in her forties. She owned one of only two convenience stores in Agades and, when I lived there, I had often bought supplies from her.

'How have you been?' I asked.

'There are no tourists,' she replied glumly. 'I want to have a strong word with Aghaly ag Alambo and tell him that it's not good enough,' she said jokingly. 'I am going to suggest that he takes a holiday!'

'As there are no tourists,' I tendered light-heartedly, 'perhaps you should all go on holiday?'

I listened to the exiles talk about the rebellion, which had effectively displaced them and put their livelihoods on hold, and heard how Agades was boarded up and overrun with militia. 'Those letters you gave me when I last saw you – I sent them at the airport in Paris,' I said to Katia, remembering she had given me some correspondence before I flew out of Agades, as I was more reliable than the local postal service.

'Thank you,' she said, but I am not sure if she remembered. I went on to explain that I had just met Issa Lamine. 'Do you want President Mamadou Tandja's number?' she asked helpfully, flicking through the pages of her little black address book.

'Not this time,' I replied. 'Thanks.'

I returned to *Les Roniers* and its canopied oasis of verdant foliage. The sandy ground was a mosaic of mottled sunlight, the air smelt of lazy hosepipe water on warm, succulent leaves, and the place was alive with the music of intermittent bird-song. I stepped into the tiny reception office to discover when I had to be at the airport and, as I did so, felt as though I had already swum out of the current of this journey. Sanda, a Djerma in his mid-sixties, sat nonchalantly behind the counter peering though a pair of glasses at the pages of a crumpled newspaper. He looked up, his chin speckled with aluminium-grey and snowy stubble, and carefully folded his paper.

'You were lucky, Monsieur Alistair, to come back alive,' he said. 'The Tubu are very dangerous.'

'That's just not true,' I answered. 'They're wonderful people.'

As I walked back out into the caressing sunlight past a bougainvillea-covered pergola I wondered exactly where my friends were at that moment, as they headed back across the Manga.

EPILOGUE

Six weeks after I returned to Britain, an article appeared on the Reuters website, reporting that: 'Tubu tribesmen' had killed several soldiers in the region of Diffa – which I passed through on my way to Nguigmi. It declared that a Tubu rebel faction had joined forces with the Tuareg MNJ and it seemed, on the face of it, as though a new front had opened up in the growing conflict between nomads and the government. The Manga, it appeared, would be shut off to foreigners. A couple of months later, the same website announced Tubu rebels had issued a warning to the government. 'China's state-owned oil company, CNPC, should not go ahead with a planned $5 billion oil investment in Niger... which included the southeast Diffa region, where CNPC signed an accord to develop the Agadem block.'

* * *

From the comfort of my Suffolk home, overlooking a pond fringed with leaning bulrushes, I kept an eye on the world news for any information about the Manga, but I saw no further bulletins from that region. I can, however, report that Zinder's governor was seriously injured by a grenade at an alleged handover of weapons by some Tuareg rebels. 'The blast killed a civilian,' I read in August 2008, 'and badly wounded the Zinder regional governor, Yahaya Yandaka, and another senior official. The government sent a plane to fly the injured to Niamey for treatment.' I have no idea if he survived, but I am grateful to him for not vetoing my journey across the Manga.

There were infrequent news snippets about aerial bombings of Tuareg villages in the Aïr and of clashes between Aghaly ag Alambo's rebels and Nigérien troops. A senior UN diplomat, Robert Fowler, was kidnapped outside Niamey and a month later, in January 2009, four more hostages – including a Briton – were seized on the Mali border with Niger. The Briton was murdered in May 2009. Later that year, in June, President Mamadou Tandja altered the constitution so that he could stay in power beyond the legal term; Issa Lamine, and other ministers, withdrew from the government in protest. Tandja was toppled in a military coup, on 18 February 2010, when soldiers stormed the Presidential Palace in broad daylight and captured him after a four-hour gun battle. The junta promised a 'return to constitutional order' and, suggesting former state officials had taken bribes from foreign mining firms, announced that 'all mining contracts would be carefully studied'.

An uneasy peace was brokered between the MNJ rebels and the Niger government towards the end of 2009, but the situation remains fragile. Niger continues to make world news each year. In 2010, it was hit by a food crisis that affected over seven million people – almost fifty per cent of the population. The country was again in the headlines after Gaddafi fugitives fled there in September 2011. And, as I write this in March 2012, another famine is looming for the Nigériens.

I know I was fortunate to have been able to cross the Manga with the Tubu, to live as they did and experience a way of life that has barely changed for centuries, and I am extremely grateful I was not ensnared in any unsavoury events beyond my control whilst there. I hope, one day, I might see my Tubu friends again. I miss them, their world and what they showed me.

GLOSSARY

Allāhu Akbar	'God is the most great'
Assalam Alaykum	'Peace be with you'
Alaykum Assalam	Reply to above: 'And upon you be peace'
Azan	The Muslim summons to prayer
FDR	Front Démocratique Révolutionnaire. A Tubu militant rebel group c.1990s
Insha'allāh	'If God is willing'
Les Anciens	The old ones, or the ancients
Marabout	A Muslim holy man
Médicins Sans Frontières	A secular humanitarian-aid NGO, known for its projects in war-torn regions and developing countries
Mosquée	Mosque
MNJ	Mouvement des Nigériens pour la Justice. A Tuareg militant rebel group (2007–9) based in Niger's Aïr Mountains.
Muezzin	The crier who calls the faithful to prayer five times a day
ṣalāt	The ritual prayer of Muslims, performed five times a day
Wossara	How are you? (Tubu)
Wossou	Good. (Reply to above)

THE CALL TO PRAYER (AZAN)

Transliteration

Allāhu Akbar
Ashhadu anna la ilāha illa Allāh
Ashhadu anna Muḥammadan rasūl Allāh
Hayya ʿalā al-ṣalāt
Hayya ʿalā al-falāḥ
Al-ṣalāt khayrun min al-nawm
Allāhu akbar
Lā ilāha illa Allāh

Translation

God is most great
I bear witness there is no God but God
I bear witness Muhammad is the prophet of God
Come to prayer
Come to well-being
Prayer is better than sleep (dawn prayer only)
God is most great
There is no God but God

RITUAL PRAYER (ṢALĀT)

Transliteration

Allāhu Akbar
Subhānaka Allāhumma wa-bi-ḥamdika wa-tabāraka ismuka
  wa-ta'āla jadduka wa-lā ilāhaghayruka
A'ūdhu bi-llāhī min al-shayṭān al-rajīm
Bismi'llāh al-raḥmān al-raḥīm
Al-ḥamdu li'llāhi rabb al-'ālamīn
Al-raḥmān al-raḥīm
Mālik yawmi'l-dīnIyyāka na'budu wa-iyyāka nasta'īn
Ihdinā al-ṣirāt al-mustaqīm
Ṣirāta alladhīna an'amta alayhim ghayr al-maghçūbi 'alayhim
  wa-lā çālīn. āmīn

[This section is a choice, but *Surat al-Ikhlāṣ* is a common choice.]
Qul huwa Allāhu aḥad
Allāhu al-ṣamad
Lam yalid wa-lam yulad
Wa-lam yakun lahu kufuwan aḥad
Ṣubḥāna rabbi al-'aẓīm
Sami'a Allāhu li-man ḥamidahu
Rabbanā laka'l-ḥamd
Ṣubḥāna rabbi al-a'lā
Al-taḥiyyātu li-llāhi wa'l-ṣalātu wa'l-ṭayyibātu
Al-salāmu 'layka ayyuha al-nabī wa-raḥmat Allāh
  wa-barakātuh
Al-salāmu 'alāynā wa-'alā 'ibād Allāh al-ṣāliḥīn
Ashhadu anna lā ilāha ilā Allāh

Wa-ashhadu anna Muḥammadan ʿabduhu wa-rasūluh
Allāhumma ṣali ʿalā Muḥammadin wa-'alā āli Muḥammadin
  kamā ṣalayta ʿalā Ibrāhīma wa-ʿalā āli Ibrāhīma innaka
  ḥamīdun majīd

Translation

God is great/most great
Glory and praise be to You, O God, Your name is blessed and
  Your power is exalted and there is no God but You
I seek refuge with God from Satan, the damned
In the name of God the Compassionate, the Merciful
Praise be to God, Lord of the worlds
The Compassionate, the Merciful
Lord of the Judgement Day
It is You we worship and You we seek help from
Show us the straight path
The path of those whom you have blessed whom you are not
  angered with
And [who are] not misguided. Amen
Say, God is one
God, the Eternal
He does not give birth or was He born
And He has no equal
Praise be to my Lord, most great
God listens to the one who praises him
O our Lord, praise to You
Praise be to my Lord, most high
Good wishes, prayers and blessing are due to God
Peace be upon you, O prophet, and the mercy and
  beneficence of God
Peace be upon us and upon God's righteous servants
I bear witness that there is no God but God and that
  Muḥammad is His servant and His messenger
O God, bless Muhammad and bless the family of
  Muhammad as you have blessed Abraham and the family
  of Abraham. Surely you are glorious and worthy of praise

MAPS

Map 1 'The Principal Caravan Routes of the Nineteenth Century' first published in E.W. Bovill *Caravans of the Sahara. An Introduction to the History of the Western Sudan* by Oxford University Press for the International Institute of African Languages & Cultures 1933. Copyright © International African Institute. Reproduced here by permission of the International African Institute, London.

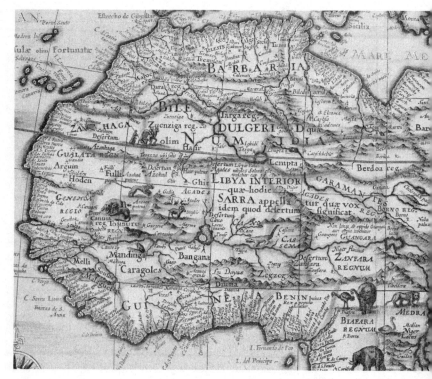

Map 2 Sahara and Northwest Africa – showing Agades – from Joan Blaeu's 1665 *Atlas Maic Africae Nova Descriptio*, Osterreichische Nationalbibliothek, Vienna, Kar 389.030 F.K. 35:03

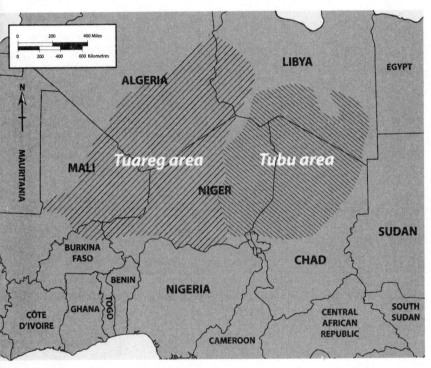

Map 3 Traditional Tuareg and Tubu regions.

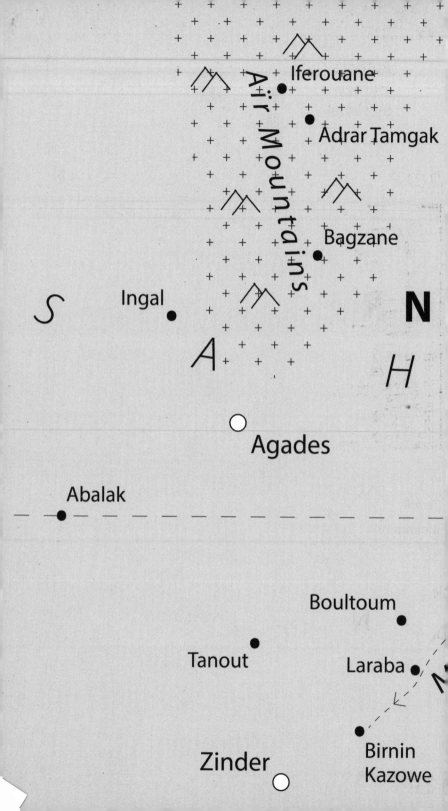